STALIN

5 year plan

☆ 12 5-34

JOSEPH STALIN

STALIN

AN IMPARTIAL STUDY OF THE LIFE AND WORK
OF
JOSEPH STALIN

By
STEPHEN GRAHAM

KENNIKAT PRESS
Port Washington, N. Y./London

STALIN

First published in 1931
Reissued in 1970 by Kennikat Press
Library of Congress Catalog Card No: 73-112803
ISBN 0-8046-1070-3

Manufactured by Taylor Publishing Company   Dallas, Texas

To

NEGLEY FARSON

MOST INTREPID OF FOREIGN CORRESPONDENTS

PREFACE

It is curious that in a long biography of Lenin such as that of Valeriu Marcu there should be only one slight reference to Stalin. It is a tribute to the ability of Stalin to keep in the background that he should have been thus overlooked. Up to a few years ago the centre of the stage had been kept by the noisier and more spectacular leaders of the revolution. Stalin has never sought publicity and the World Press comment on his doings must have been many times less than that of Trotsky.

No doubt the Western Press is at this moment making up for its deficiency. Since Stalin rose to be the supreme personal power in Soviet Russia many articles have been written on his life and significance. Even these have been lacking in detail. That is because few correspondents have even spoken to him. He avoids interviews and it is, on the surface, difficult to glean information about his past or his career.

For that reason I have written this *Life* of Stalin, to supply a need. We ought to know more about the man who is successfully promulgating the Five Year Plan for Russia, the man with whose will and judgment the whole destiny of Russia is at present linked.

Lenin was the brains of the revolution, but he was a sick man and had not the physical energy necessary for the realisation of his theory of Socialism. Trotsky was Lenin's town crier, not much more than that, though possessed of great conceit. Stalin is the man of sagacity and will who has carried the revolution on to its present stage.

The story of his youthful adventures, his great part in the Civil War, his idolatry of Lenin, the drama of his struggle for power with Trotsky, and of his complete triumph over all rivals within the Communist Party give the measure of a remarkable personality. In some respects he must be regarded to-day as a greater man than Lenin.

STEPHEN GRAHAM.

CHAPTER I

GEORGIA, until the rise of Stalin, had produced no great man of affairs, no striking figure in world history. It has a history as a kingdom, extending over two thousand years, but the chief features in that history are the invasion and conquest by those great ravagers, Alexander, Genghis Khan and Tamerlane. One monarch of the country attained a legendary fame, the dark Tamara who entertained and murdered her lovers in the castle in the Gorge of Dariel. The territory of Georgia is the Caucasus Mountains, the mighty snow-crowned range which symbolically divides Europe from her Aryan origins.

Russia absorbed Georgia at the beginning of the nineteenth century. The tribes of the Caucasus rebelled under the leadership of the heroic Shamyl, not a Georgian, at the time of the Crimean War, but they were dispersed without much difficulty. Following upon pacification some fine Russian regiments were raised in Georgia, for the race produces the most handsome men in the world. The men are unusually tall; the women, short and full-breasted, do not correspond to a Western standard of beauty.

The fire of local patriotism still burned in the Georgians but they were nevertheless loyal subjects of the Tsars. There was never a revolutionary ferment comparable to that of Poland, the Baltic Provinces and Finland. Tiflis, the capital, became more famous for good cooking than for anything else in the world. Kakhetinsky wine and the *shashlik* stood instead of Georgia. And yet Georgia has produced Stalin.

9

He was born south of the range at Gori, a little town on the railway going from Tiflis to Batum. His real name is Joseph Djugashvilli, his childish nickname which has endured was Soso; but he took the name of Koba and after that became Nizheradze. Then he became Chizhikof and at another time Ivanovitch. Lenin is said to have suggested to him his final fighting alias, Stalin, which means the man of steel.

Stalin's father was a bootmaker in Gori. One writer tells how impressed the little boy was, comparing the dandy shoes of the rich which came in for repair with the rough gear of the poor. But that is probably nonsense. Later on his father left this one-man business to become a genuine proletarian, working in the Adelkhanof factory in Tiflis. Stalin's mother was an Ossetine peasant who could neither read nor write and did not speak Russian. She had other boys but they died in childhood. Joseph was the much-prized only surviving son. The father died before the boy reached puberty, so one may assume the mother as the stronger influence. Physically Stalin derived more from his mother than from his father. He is not a characteristic Georgian. He is short, fleshy, muscular; he has the deep-set eyes of a thinker, the thick curved eyebrows which one associates with an oriental haggler and bargainer. His face at rest is massive, his expression impenetrable. He called himself the steel man, but "stone-face" would not have been inappropriate.

The Ossetines from whom Stalin derived on his mother's side are a tribe altogether more barbarous and violent than the Georgians. That they have racial connection with the Finns and the Magyars

has not made them Europeans. They are just an
illiterate, wild mountain clan.

The date of Stalin's birth is 1879. That was in the
reign of Alexander the Liberator. The serfs had been
freed, but that did not affect Stalin's parents, as the
Caucasus was not enslaved. The insurrection of the
tribes had long since been quelled, and the policy of
Russification was developing. Russia had greatly
extended her sway in South-western Asia by the
annexation of Khiva, Bokhara, Samarkand. A blow
had also been struck at Turkish power in the Balkans;
Serbia, Bulgaria and Rumania had re-emerged in
history. Then Alexander II, one of the greatest of
the Tsars, was blown to bits by Sophia Perovskaya
on the quay of the Catherine Canal in St. Petersburg.
It is said that he had a draft of a Constitution for
Russia under consideration for his signature at the
time. If so it was premature; for Russia was at that
time in no way fitted for Parliamentary government.
Liberals frequently are murdered while tyrants die
in their beds. Alexander III took revenge on the
people of the Empire for the assassination of his
father but he met with no violent end.

The adolescence of Stalin corresponds to the
unsympathetic rule of Alexander II, which was
a progressive ferment of petty nationalism and
nihilism. The boy was educated at a free school,
taught by a priest in Gori. His parents were poor,
but to some extent ambitious for their child. It was
common enough for children to languish in illiteracy
in those parts. But Djugashvilli, the cobbler, decided
that he would like to have his son become a priest.
Joseph was not slow to learn what he was taught,
but he probably learned more in the mountains

minding sheep, riding and chasing horses. That was how he spent most of his free time. And he had his own gang of boys up there and was their leader. While he was being trained to be a priest he was training himself to be a robber. In the Caucasus to be a robber is to be something of a hero. Bandits are held in awe and honour, and there are whole tribes, such as the Ingush, who vaunt their white hands, living cleanly and honourably by horse-stealing. And it is nobler to kill a man than to talk about it.

When he had been three years at the elementary school at Gori he passed to the theological seminary at Tiflis, and his mother moved to Tiflis with him. He moved from a small town where the cattle came in from pasture along the main street in the evening to a metropolis of 250,000 souls, to theatres, clubs, cafés, newspapers and street-bred youth, further from the wild mountains, nearer to Europe and civilisation. In the imbroglio of youthful Tiflis he speedily went astray, imbibed Georgian nationalism and revolutionary fervour. While studying his Byzantine books which demand so much of one's credulity, he read Karl Marx as well. Logic and materialism won an easy victory over gnosticism and when the head of the seminary expelled him as unsuitable for the priesthood he was only confirming a decision which had already been taken in Stalin's mind. Within a few months of his exclusion he joined the Tiflis branch of the Social Democratic party.

He was then nineteen years of age and had definitely become a revolutionary. For the S.D. party had barely the right to exist. Its organisation was secret

and its members came automatically under the
secret supervision of the police.

Now the reactionary Alexander was dead and had
been suceeded by the weak Tsar Nicholas II.
Nicholas was too much occupied with his bride and
his domestic bliss to pay much attention to personal
government, and autocracy degenerated into bureau-
cracy, which meant a very considerable increase in
police activity and military political supervision.
During his reign all the national minorities were
progressively stirred toward revolution. The party
grew rapidly in Tiflis, Baku and Batum, making
very successful propaganda among the factory
hands, the workers in the oil industry and the
railwaymen.

Two years after joining the party Stalin joined its
executive and began to direct its activities. At that
time there was not a great deal of scope. There was
no expectation of an armed rising. All that was
practicable was the printing of illicit pamphlets and
their distribution among the working class, the
roping in of new members and the raising of
funds for the work and for the defence of arrested
members. The party was poor. Prisoners were
sometimes approached by delegations and offered
fifty copecks, or one rouble, toward the cost of
defence.

It was a dull time in Russian history. There were
no wars. There was suppression of individual
liberties; there was much censorship of the colourless Press; there was Russification of national minorities; under the fanatical Pobedonostsef there was
violent anti-semitism. But the Russians themselves,
who outnumbered by ten to one the minorities of

the Empire, were passive. Partly due to the influence of Dostoievsky Russia's belief in herself had become stronger, and there was more than a little national indifference toward the Poles, Jews, Letts, Finns, Esthonians, Tartars, Georgians with which the empire was embarrassed.

According to Karl Marx, Capitalism held in it the seeds of its own destruction. It was bound to collapse whether there were a revolutionary movement or not. Revolution must come; it was part of the historical process. At the same time, at the end of the twentieth century it did not look as if it were coming at all speedliy. For of course Marx was looking for world-revolution and was not merely envisaging a local upset such as a change of regime in Russia. Stalin, at least, was discontented with the prospect "History must be given a shove."

Tiflis itself was a remote place in which to work for world-revolution. In most maps of the world it is shewn as in Asia rather than in Europe. "God is high and the Tsar is far away," was a common enough thought in Tiflis. Transcaucasia was an obscure region to which not much political attention was given. Thither migrated Molokans, Baptists and other sectarians in order to be immune from persecution. The excommunication of Count Tolstoy in 1901 for his Protestant religious teaching caused no little stir in Tiflis, but that meant little to Stalin who had abjured religion, both evangelical and sacramental. Revolution was a matter of economic cause and effect: that was his bedrock of belief. It must come: that was Marx. It could be hastened by action: that was Lenin and his disciple Stalin.

Stalin heard of Lenin years before he met him and worshipped him from afar. Lenin, alone among all revolutionary leaders and thinkers, appealed to him. In 1900 Lenin came straight from Siberia to revolutionary work and organisation in Switzerland. His strong will and decided personality at once made themselves felt among the political émigrés. He was a born leader of men. He began at once to make his own party and to winnow the revolutionaries for men who could be his helpers. He never looked for numbers of adherents, but for quality and individual strength, holding that mere table-talk gets one nowhere in a revolution.

The revolutionary newspaper *Iskra*, the Spark, just started in Geneva, brought the personality of Lenin to Tiflis. Pamphlets by Lenin followed. The vigorous new writer wished to put the Social Democratic party into training, get rid of the fat and the flesh and the sentimentalism and make a party which should be all muscle and will. Some tension between old and young comrades in Switzerland was apparent in the articles and brochures. Stalin was naturally attracted to the flag-bearer of youth. Then a friend of Lenin's came to Tiflis, one Kurnatovsky, and brought with him an infectious enthusiastic heroworship. Ardent youth craves leadership and it seemed to Stalin that the Revolution had found its true leader. Stalin had found his.

All Lenin's efforts were directed so that his "Spark" should not smoke like a dirty lamp, that it should burst into flame so that people afar in Russia should see it clearly. "Yes, that's it," said Stalin. "It must not smoke. He understands. He's an extraordinary man."

Stalin called Lenin the "mountain eagle of the party."

There was nothing physically magnificent about Lenin. He was more a buzzard than an eagle, but he had vision and pounce. Apart from his youthful hero-worship that is what Stalin meant. The eagle knows when and where to strike. Lenin added nothing to Marxism beyond tactics. If upon occasion he stated the theory of the proletarian revolution in a new way, that also was tactics. In Lenin's mind the end justified any means, and that freedom from moral prejudice and convention appealed to Stalin, who possessed that type of mental and moral outfit. Stalin had a little more. Lenin had freedon of conscience; Stalin had freedom of conscience plus a will to use that freedom vigorously.

In the autumn of 1901 the Social Democratic Committee in Tiflis was raided and "Koba" Stalin went into hiding in the mountains. When the danger of arrest became less he went over to Batum on the coast and organised a committee there and led the strikes in the Rothschild and Mantashef factories. In February, 1902, he had a part in anti-governmental demonstrations in the city and was seized by the police. He then spent twenty months in prison and at the end of that time was banished for three years to Eastern Siberia. Thus, at the age of twenty-four, his revolutionary activity received, as it were, an official certificate from the police. The police did involuntary service to the leaders of the revolutionary party abroad by sorting out the active spirits.

And Stalin was not only sufficiently important to be banished to Siberia but he showed his metal by escaping at once. No sooner was he set down in Novaya Uda, in the province of Irkutsk, than he disappeared. He gave his guards the slip, got on a freight train and in a very short time turned up at his mother's house to supper.

CHAPTER II

THE hope of the revolutionaries was war. Lenin freely confessed that a rising of the peasantry with sticks and stones could not overthrow the Tsardom. Leaflets would not overthrow it. Strikes, even a general strike, could not succeed. A minority could only seize power by a *coup d'état*, but while rifles and ammunition were for the most part safely stored a *coup* was impracticable. But a disgruntled and undisciplined soldiery returning from an unsuccessful war might supply the means. Lenin never dreamed of converting a majority of the Russian people to Communism. The democratic conception of majority rule was far from his mind. Hence his contempt for Parliamentarism, the Duma, the Constituent Assembly. The mountain eagle's view was this: when the right moment comes, a determined band of men can snatch the power of the government and make the sort of revolution they desire. So when Nicholas II embarked on the folly of the Japanese War hope stirred in Geneva. And when that war was attended by great disaster, Lenin became of opinion that Russia was "pregnant with the revolution."

It was in this time of pregnancy that Stalin met Lenin first. The Russians, unlike Germans or British, are not a people who stand by their leaders in time of catastrophe. The Tsardom was bankrupt of credit because of the débâcle in Manchuria, and great numbers of people, especially young people, were on tiptoe to welcome revolution. There were strikes, disorders, mutinies in many parts. The Tsar's hand was forced; he granted a Constitution. But that did not satisfy the neurotic impulse for change.

Stalin had come from the Caucasus to Tammerfors, in Finland, for a conference with Lenin and other revolutionary leaders. He came from scenes of disorder, the most sinister of which was the Tartar-Armenian race riot in Baku. This riot gave the Russians a pretext to terrorise the mixed population of the streets of Baku. In the mountains the tribesmen were restive but the government, by the aid of Cossacks, was showing them who was master. It would be untrue to say that Stalin was boiling with indignation. When excited he gets cooler. He approved the tactics: force was the only thing that people understood. Had the government sent down some talkative Parliamentarians to appease the Caucasus nothing would have been effected.

For that reason he was opposed to any participation of the revolutionaries in the Duma. Force must be answered by force. Stalin stood up and addressed the Conference and in the conference—Lenin. "No agreements and no compromises," he demanded. "Either we win now or we never win. Consider it well; the government has shed much blood throughout the land. Now it mocks the general demands of the people by granting a constitutional assembly. The Duma decree is an attempt on the part of the government to deceive the peasantry and the proletariat and to postpone its final destruction. Does not that decree exclude the proletariat and the mass of the peasantry from participation in the elections. How can we revolutionaries find any basis of agreement in that decree? No. The one answer of the class conscious proletariat is resolute opposition to this forgery of the popular will. We must break this police Duma and reject all part in it. We can use the occasion of the ballot not for voting but for the extension of the revolutionary organisation of the proletariat and to stir all sections of the people to armed rising. A rising—that is the one way out at present. It must at once be prepared for and organised everywhere. Only by victory in such a rising will it be possible to create a real popular government. And so—no agreement, but war. Let us have an armed rising!"

There were cheers even from those who did not agree. That, at least, was the right spirit. In the intervals between speeches some of the delegates went to musketry practice. Lenin is said to have noted Stalin as a coming man. He may or he may not. At least he nodded approval. But there was nothing remarkable about Stalin's speech. There are always hot-heads who will call for a fight. There could have been very little chance of victory in an armed struggle with the forces of the Tsar. The army had not been sufficiently undermined for that. Still it was Lenin's opinion that it was better to strike against great odds than to be lost in a sea of political verbiage.

Nevertheless, Lenin did not plan an armed rising, neither in 1905 nor in 1917, but was ready to step in and take advantage of one should it succeed. At the conference of Tammerfors in December, 1905, the insurrection was neither planned nor predicted. The news of the rising came next morning and took the delegates by surprise. So, in truth, while they

were still talking about it the red youth of Moscow
were raising the barricades.

Revolution flared like cordite in the streets of
Moscow. The Governor was taken by surprise.
The gendarmerie was inadequate. The garrison
wavered. At first it seemed as if the revolutionaries
might gain possession of the city. Lenin and the
rest, disguised and with false passports rushed to
St. Petersburg, ready to take control if the revolt
should become general. Their immediate task was
to prevent reinforcements being sent to the Moscow
garrison. Some of the delegates were for raising a
similar revolt in St. Petersburg and thus occupying
the attention of the troops stationed there long
enough to allow the revolutionaries of Moscow to
gain control. Others thought it enough to sever
railway communication between Moscow and St.
Petersburg. The railwaymen were out on strike and
train service between the two cities was suspended.

The revolutionaries sounded the rank and file of
the regiments in St. Petersburg, the factory workers,
the students, but found no response. Only the
workers from the explosive factories were ready to
come out, and a few hundred sailors could be set
on to start a riot. It was decided to form a battalion
of railwaymen and raid an arsenal. There was a
scarcity of weapons. The news came in that the
government intended to restaff the Moscow-St.
Petersburg railway with military and run a series
of relief trains. Lenin was too late. The permanent
way had nowhere been destroyed. Deputations were
sent to the troops to dissuade them from railway
service. In the dark they mingled with the men at
arms and argued with them all night even to zero

hour but all to no avail. The soldiers did not denounce them to their officers, but they were surly and unsympathetic. Even though conscious of wrongs, and discontented for many reasons, they were still under control and had no desire to risk being shot at dawn. The deputations, worn out and discouraged, brought their empty tidings to the breakfast table. Troop trains bristling with arms had already steamed south from the sidings of St. Petersburg.

Before noon the Semenovsky and Ladozhky regiments had arrived in Moscow and the city was saved for the Tsar.

Stalin, who had taken little active part in all this, was savage. "What a way to prepare for Revolution," he exclaimed. "Words, words, words, when only arms and action were needed."

"Never mind," said Lenin quietly. "We have had a terrible lesson. We shall do better next time."

The new regiments soon cleaned up the Moscow streets. The revolution fled indoors. The police entered and made their manifold arrests. The barricades were pushed to the sidewalks. The shops re-opened. The trams started again.

It was a decisive blow. The revolution was counted out at Moscow. Some thought it had still the power to rise and fight again, but they were mistaken. Peace ensued. Still there were assassinations and many pitiful murders of petty police officers in Warsaw. But organised revolt had been struck to the ground and never raised its head again until the middle of the Great War, March, 1917. The revolutionaries were forced back to their books and their pamphlets.

CHAPTER III

THE Social Democratic Party was in any case divided against itself. Some wanted more and were Bolsheviks; some wanted less and were Mensheviks, The Bolsheviks were for victory or nothing; the Mensheviks believed in the inevitability of gradualness. The Bolsheviks remained militant; the Mensheviks entered the Russian parliamentary struggle and allied themselves with the Constitutional Democrats or, as they were called for short, the Cadets, by no means a revolutionary party. At that time the Bolsheviks and Mensheviks, though destined to become mortal enemies, were accommodated within one party. At the ensuing conference of Stockholm in 1906 the Mensheviks outvoted the Bolsheviks, and Lenin found himself with the minority.

In the election of the central committee of the Party neither Lenin nor Stalin were successful. The majority of the committee was Menshevik. It is true that Krassin and Rikof were elected; they were of Lenin's faction, but they were neither of them militant in temperament. Neither Rikof nor Krassin was representative of the vigour and force of Lenin.

It is interesting to look forward eleven years to the beginnings of the Revolution in 1917–18. The Mensheviks, as the natural inheritors of the power of the Duma, got into the saddle first. But the Bolsheviks had force and leadership and so easily displaced them.

Lenin and Trotsky and Stalin were far from submission to the will of the majority in 1906. As a minority the Bolsheviks preserved their individuality, and under the leadership of Lenin organised themselves as a party of strength. The problem was not to try in the first place for numbers but to win over from the Menshevik faction the younger and more active members. In this Lenin was successful. The co-operation with the Duma gave ample opportunity for scornful and telling criticism. When in the following year at London the next conference was held the Bolsheviks turned the tables on the Mensheviks and obtained the control of the party as a whole. This control they never lost till the clash with the Mensheviks at the beginning of the Revolution.

But the actual prospect of revolution in Russia rapidly faded. The Tsar himself might be weak but he had at his command capable statesmen such as Witte, Stolypin, Kokovtsef. The effect of the Japanese war was rapidly obliterated. It was said that Russia had lost the war but she had won the peace and got more advantage through the Treaty of Portsmouth than she could have obtained before mobilisation. Western Europe, moreover, did not wish revolution, especially France. If there should be revolution where would be the sacred alliance and the capital of the French bondholders? The inauguration of the Duma had also obtained British sympathy for Russia. Belief in the stability of Russian institutions grew rapidly in London. The cities obtained loans from British banks. England bought or supported Russian railways and British capital began eventually to surge into Russia. Almost the whole material influence of the West was in the balance against a change of regime. And Russia

herself moved along the road of prosperity and
picked up hope and belief in herself as she moved.

The numbers of the revolutionaries rapidly
declined; the funds at their disposal diminished.
The emigrés held their annual conferences and
discussed points of political strategy, but they were
merely a small bunch of bitter and disgruntled
politicians who talked with heat. The worst aspect
of their position seemed lack of funds. Professional
revolutionaries must live. The sort of journalism
they did was poorly paid, and funds were necessary
for printing newspapers and pamphlets. It was
more difficult, after 1916, to obtain subscriptions
from rich sympathisers. The comrades were too poor
to raise much among themselves.

The chief hope of finance seemed to lie in "expropriation," if it could be compassed. "Expropriation"
was a common word in those days, a euphemism
for practical banditry, more practised in the Caucasus
than in any other part of Russia. Stalin said to
Lenin: "I will get you money."

"How?"

"Expropriation."

Lenin and Stalin discussed a plan which resulted
in the most daring exploit of Stalin's youth.

The robbery which he undertook has been used
considerably to defame Stalin. But there seems no
reason why an isolated act of political banditry
should be considered more heinous than the mass
expropriations which were carried out later in the
course of the revolution.

On the 13th June, 1917, the Tiflis branch of the
State bank was to have received from St. Petersburg
341,000 roubles, a bulky package of 642 five-hundred

rouble notes.[1] The cashier, Kurdumof, had these with him in an open cab. A second vehicle followed him with four armed guards. They were escorted by a detachment of Cossacks. As they approached the Governor's house a big bomb was thrown by one of the band organised by Stalin, some say by Stalin himself. The big bomb explosion was followed by a number of smaller ones and several men standing about opened fire on the convoy with revolvers. There was a panic and the cashier fell out of the cab. Off dashed the horses like mad but another conspirator successfully exploded a bomb under them as they galloped. They were killed and the cab stopped. The thrower of this last bomb, "Kamo" Petrosyan, dashed in and seized the package of notes which the cashier had abandoned. He jumped into a fast-going mountain cart, and still firing at the Cossacks as he went, he made his escape. The convoy, at sixes and sevens, did not make a single arrest, and Stalin's band got off scot-free,—with the plunder. There was a considerable number of casualties among the Cossacks, who were badly led and did not even give chase after the right people. Lenin got his money. Stalin, it is said, did not touch a penny of it. However, according to one writer, the Bolsheviks only admit receiving 250,000 roubles.[2]

If the Bolsheviks only received 250,000 roubles, may it not be conjectured that the party in Transcaucasia also got an accession of funds?

The series of the notes was known, A.M. 62900-63541 and all banks in Russia were warned to be

[1] Figures of the *Novoe Vremy*.
[2] M. A. Aldanof: *Sovremenniki*, p. 112.

on the look-out for them. But the notes did not turn up within the confines of the Empire. "Papa" Litvinof was stopped at Paris trying to change some of them.

The comrades then went to London to confer, and Stalin joined Lenin there. Some of them took part in the open-air meetings in Hyde Park. In truth Stalin went to Lenin rather than to the conference. He wished to defeat Menshevism, but of conferences, as such, he had not a high opinion. He remained a staunch believer in Lenin but the rest of the delegates struck him as ineffectual. They in their turn did not think much of him. He was dirty and untidy in his dress and habits. His personality seemed Asiatic and greasy. They did not like his Georgian accent and his dog-like fidelity to Lenin. Doubtless no one looked upon him as a coming great man. That is a curiosity of Stalin's career. Until he actually won everything and became dictator of Russia, most ambitious revolutionaries thought him a man in a secondary rôle. Zinovief called him a Caucasus monkey with yellow eyes. To Trotsky he was merely a native, one of the savages who live in the Caucasus. For Trotsky had a Jewish pride in being Western and civilised. He had been a waiter and no doubt an excellent one at that.

The life of the uncouth Stalin was one of continual adventure and struggle, very different from that of the white-handed delegates to the conferences. After the London conference in 1907 he returned to Baku where he founded a paper for Lenin. Next year, in March, he was arrested and put in prison. After eight months' imprisonment he was banished to the easy-going Northern province of Vologda. He fled, returned to the mountains, only to be arrested again and sent back. The government was becoming much more lenient toward the revolutionaries. In earlier years he would probably have been executed. But the Tsardom was no longer in danger and could afford to look upon revolutionaries more as political freaks than as enemies of the state.

Stalin fled a second time from Vologda and this time went to St. Petersburg to see what he could do there. Again he was arrested and sent back to his place of banishment in Vologda. He escaped again, and again went to St. Petersburg. That was in January, 1912. He was arrested again in April and banished for four years to Narim. But the police could not hold him. He displayed a genius for escape. Hardly had he been put down in the desolate region of banishment than he had disappeared. While the police were still seeking him in Russia he had already crossed the frontier and was sitting having tea with Lenin in Cracow.

Lenin was greatly impressed with the adventures of Stalin, his energy and indefatigability in the cause of revolution. He saw to it that Stalin was rewarded. Against the will of other prominent revolutionaries, he had Stalin adopted into the central committee of the Party. He thus became one of the leaders of the Bolsheviks and ceased to be merely a provincial delegate. But for him it was not decorative: he never wore his success as Trotsky did. He was a worker. Invested with greater authority, he returned to St. Petersburg, there to advise a line of action to the Social Democrats in the Duma. There were in 1912 two Bolshevik newspapers running in St. Petersburg, the oft-suppressed *Pravda*, revived again, and the *Zvezda*. These were directed by Lenin from Cracow, and Stalin came to them with the authority of Lenin to write what he liked there. Stalin was becoming a fairly effective journalist and pamphleteer. He had a fine, clear, direct style which goes much to disprove his alleged intellectual dullness.

He lived very much as a bachelor. His consumptive first wife, in the Caucasus, he never saw again. He had no home life. The comrades looked after his children as best they could. The father's whole life interest and energy was given to the cause of revolution. A man of so many aliases, changes of abode, imprisonments and banishments could not very well fulfill his part either as husband or father.

In the spring of 1913 he was arrested again. He was banished to a remoter part of Eastern Siberia and this time was properly guarded. His repeated attempts to escape were frustrated and he remained in durance for four years, only to be liberated as a result of the revolution. Therefore, despite his great activity, it cannot be said that Stalin did so very much to bring about the actual catastrophe in Russia. He came in, like so many others, when the Tsardom was already stricken, and used the opportunity provided by the political chaos which ensued after the events of March, 1917.

CHAPTER IV

STALIN arriving in Petrograd at the beginning of April, 1917, was greatly bewildered by the revolution. What he had been striking against had fallen in ruins. As a personality in the revolution he seemed to have lost significance. The Mensheviks, with their policy of co-operation in the political struggle, seemed to have it all their own way. They were even ousting from power their allies the Cadets. Except for the confused clamour of the newly established soviets of soldier and workmen delegates, Bolshevism as such seemed to have no voice or part in the great affair.

One sees a man of considerable will and subtlety almost devoid of political vision. He was no Napoleon who could see in a trice the strategical significance in the disposition of forces. He rushed about like an ant with its head cut off. None of those in power recognised in him a man of any significance. He was just one of the many returning from exile and prison, no doubt nursing pretensions to recompense which could not be satisfied.

It has been said that his theological training taught him to seek dogma. He must have a Bible in which to seek guidance and authority. In later years he certainly put the seal of sacred writ upon Lenin's writings and elaborated Communism into a Church. To put it briefly and vulgarly Lenin was his god. Only when Lenin returned to Russia did he begin to find himself in the revolution.

The Germans conveyed Lenin over the frontier as an act of war. Their action was in no sense prompted by political sympathy. The sealed wagon was as much an engine of destruction as Big Bertha or poison gas. It was shrewdly calculated that Lenin could make the revolution still worse by aggravating the disorganisation of the national forces of Russia. This was one of the rare occasions in which the Germans were sound of judgment in a matter of international psychology. In a sense they understood the situation better than Lenin himself. For Lenin, approaching the Russian frontier, had considerable apprehension that he would be at once arrested. Zinovief who was with him was yellow with fright.

The dumbfounding oratory of Kerensky was confusing everybody. Not for the first time a vehement vocabulary was mistaken for strength. It is possible to do an injustice to Kerensky. No one knows what was his secret intention in the early months of the revolution. He was as Machiavellian as Lenin himself, if less gifted. It is possible that while obtaining a renewal of credits from England and crying "On with the war!" he intended at his convenience to wind up the Russian campaign, make a separate peace on good terms and inaugurate a Socialist republic on moderate lines. Up to the date of the revolution he had been an unmistakable pacifist and defeatist. And although he attempted to fraternise with the Tsar in bondage he was one of the most poisonous enemies the Tsardom ever had. He was at heart more of a dictator than a constitutionalist, and never intended the Constituent Assembly to assemble. Then of course he got swell-headed and drunk with his own words.

If Kerensky intended to continue a national war

on Germany he must have viewed with suspicion the *laisser aller* granted to Lenin and other revolutionaries by the German government. It would not have been difficult to have them arrested as spies or at least as agents in the German pay. Indeed, rumour grew that Lenin was indeed a spy whose object was the betrayal of Russia, and for that reason, three months after he came he was obliged to flee the country in disguise.

But sentimentality ruled. Lenin, Zinovief and the rest were let in, and despite the fact that Lenin had again to flee, he had time to make his plans and organise the Bolsheviks within Russia. When, in April, 1917, Lenin got out of the close-shuttered train there was a deputation to meet him from the Soldiers' and Workmen's Soviets and it was led by Kamenef and Stalin. The workmen and soldiers, all wearing red rosettes, shouldered their leader and bore him triumphantly from the railway station. A part of Petrograd which seemed like the whole was waiting to welcome him as a returning hero. He was to enjoy, as it were, a Roman triumph. Pressing a bouquet of red carnations to his waistcoat like an embarrassed and blushing prima donna he listened to the exaggerated phrases of a young naval lieutenant. Quite possibly he had the man executed later on, but he murmured "Now really!" and reserved his judgment.

Chkheidze, a Georgian who had apparently found his feet in the revolution, made a speech on behalf of the Provisional Government, hoping for loyal co-operation on the part of Lenin, to which Lenin replied with the slogan: "Long live the social revolution!"

Stalin was watching his leader closely. Lenin, though non-committal, was not lost as he had been. He was observant, he was silent, but his silence was pregnant.

The tumultuous gathering was shouting. It was welcoming Lenin but it was also voicing the popular demands. The Soviet as an alternative organ of government had continued its sittings all the while since the Duma took control. It demanded things which the Provisional Government did not intend to grant: "Down with the war!", "The Land for the people!", "Give us bread; nationalise our food!"

In conversation with Stalin afterwards Lenin said: "We associate ourselves with all the popular demands. The people have made the revolution: we will carry out the popular will. First of all we stand for immediate peace with Germany and the freedom of the rank and file to return home forthwith.

It certainly sounded as if he were an agent of Germany, but that thought did not enter Stalin's mind, who knew well enough that Lenin could be no one's agent but his own.

Joseph Djugashvilli was attentive. He had received guidance from his oracle. The tactic seems simple enough as set down here after the event, but Stalin accepted it not simply for the moment but in the shape of a formula for his career as a politician. It may be stated in another form: Originate nothing! Find out what the majority intends to have and then stand up quietly and advise it as your own original judgment.

Stalin had his cue and the evolution had its turn. As agitators Stalin and his comrades were well trained, and after all what was required at the moment was intensified agitation among the workmen and the soldiers. If properly roused to the danger of their losing the liberty which the revolution seemed to have given them they could be made to oust the Provisional Government from power. Discontent was the greatest potential factor in the situation.

"We are going to have not half a revolution but a whole revolution." Lenin's policy was not without danger to those who espoused it. The odium of a German invasion of the country might fall upon them. It seemed safer to seem to uphold Kerensky. Kamenef, Zinovief, Tomsky, Dzherzhinsky were all at first opposed to Lenin's policy. Almost his sole supporter of any note was Stalin. But the younger element and the mob supported him. It was possible to organise propagandist units. Little soviets, Bolshevik nuclei, cells as they were called, appeared like maggots in every living organism of the country. And Stalin bred them. When in July Lenin was obliged to go into hiding in Finland he could leave the scene of action with the assurance that forces had been set at work which would enable him to return and lead the Bolshevik movement to complete triumph.

His progress was made easier by the mistakes of Kerensky, who abolished capital punishment, thus facilitating lynch law and lawlessness. Kerensky also played into his hands by abolishing the salute and allowing committees of the rank and file to supplant the authority of officers. It is true that the treachery and foolishness of Kerensky brought into being another danger, a powerful national force under the command of Kornilof, but that, though ultimately menacing to the soviets, was also an embarrassment of the Provisional Government. Had there been no Lenin organising from Finland, Kornilof would have swept Kerensky from power and set up a National Military Government.

Trotsky arrived in Petrograd in May. He had set off from New York on the first of April, but his boat put in at Halifax, Nova Scotia, the passengers were revised by the British police and Trotsky was placed under arrest, pending instructions from London. Only with difficulty and after a month's delay did he get permission to resume his voyage to the country of the revolution. He was a little late, some weeks later than Lenin and Zinovief, but he came in on the crest of the wave and at once became extremely active. His activity was chiefly a matter of turbulent speech-making and stirring up audiences of working men and soldiers. But when Lenin and Zinovief went into hiding he remained on the scene of action. It was a time of beating up the Bolsheviks who were openly declared to be counter-revolutionaries by the Provisional Government. Trotsky says that Stalin at the time "simply let events slide, hoping that they might show their wisdom the day after." It is not clear that Trotsky himself did more. It was not Trotsky and Stalin who were hastening the day of the Bolshevik revolution but the incapable Kerensky.

Lenin saw that the fall of Kerensky was inevitable and that it was going to be a question who should succeed him, Kornilof or the soviets. Kornilof was organising his national army and threatening to seize the capital. The Bolsheviks had the advantage of having the capital as their main stronghold. That advantage was, however, imperilled from another angle. It was possible that the Germans would be allowed to take Petrograd and capture the whole central organisation of the Party. Lenin in September 1917, wrote to the executive committee in Petrograd: "The Bolsheviks now *can* and *must* take the power of government into their own hands."

That was Lenin's comment on an ultimatum which had been sent to Kerensky by Kornilof supported by several divisions of cavalry. "At the approach of the cavalry to Petrograd, the masses rose as one man to defend the revolutionary capital. The Bolsheviks were foremost in organising the defence, and their prestige made a tremendous leap upwards. The masses saw that they were the only party whose leaders had not dallied with counter-revolution."[1]

Lenin's message was addressed personally to Stalin as to his most faithful henchman. It was followed by another in similar terms. Stalin was requested to place Lenin's advice before the committee of the Party for discussion. But there was considerable opposition. Kamenef was strongly opposed to action. It took him a long while to grasp that he was not going to be the great man of the revolution. Zinovief was also opposed to it. Later, Lenin mentioned this fact to the discredit of Kamenef and Zinovief in his last will and testament to the Party when he died. But Trotsky also was for delay. Trotsky had been elected president of the Petrograd Soviet; he was the official figurehead of the whole soviet movement and for a moment, possibly, his power and authority seemed to eclipse that of Lenin. He was for achieving the new revolution politically rather than violently, by acclamation rather than by show

[1] D. S. Mirsky; *Lenin.*

of bayonet. He therefore delayed action until the Second General Congress of Soviets of All Russia fixed for October 25th.

The *coup d'état* was not dangerous. Kerensky fled. Repin, who was painting him, went for his last sitting to the Winter Palace, but Kerensky was not there. The painter wandered from room to room in the palace and there were no guards anywhere. Priceless art-treasures and ornaments of gold and silver were still in the rooms and not a soul to protect them if the mob chose to break in.

"There was a moment," said the aged painter to me when I met him afterwards, "when the power of the Tsars lay in the dirt of the streets like a fallen jewel, and no one picked it up."

The Bolsheviks won, not in a battle but in a demonstration. The *canaille* of the city went looting, but in effect the leaders merely marched in and took up the reins of government.

Stalin took an active part in the preparation for the Bolshevik demonstration of power. The central committee of the Party nominated seven of its number as a commission to organise and arm their adherents. The seven were Lenin, Trotsky, Kamenef, Zinovief, Stalin, Sokolnikof, Bubnof. They became in due course the *Politbureau*. Dzherzhinsky and Uritsky acted as part of an auxiliary militant committee.

A new government was formed called The Soviet of People's Commissaries, the *Sovnarkom*, and it was composed entirely of Bolsheviks. Again Zinovief and Kamenef were in opposition to their leader and wished to make a coalition government of various shades of socialist politicians, including Social-

Revolutionaries and Mensheviks. But Lenin over-
ruled them. Now he was there in their midst he
had the will and the prestige which enabled him to
control the situation. Lenin made many speeches
in those days. All made speeches except Stalin,
who smoked his pipe and was silent. "In all this
I am but a small man," said he with conviction.
He was more at ease in the company of Lenin than
with the Jewish leaders of the revolution. He took
little part in the wild discussions of the time. He
had simplified his mind and his will by the formula:
"What Lenin says will be law." He was content
to be the personal runner and servant of Lenin. It
commonly became his rôle to convey the wishes of
Lenin to others. He might be called the spearhead
of Lenin's will.

But in these early days Stalin did not visibly
increase the importance. It was the hour of Trotsky
who with orations almost overshadowed Lenin himself. Three very ambitious men had entered in a
race for power, Trotsky, Kamenef, Zinovief. Not
that they entertained any idea of displacing Lenin
himself. But every sultan needs a grand vizier. In
this race Stalin had the appearance of a complete
outsider. His crafty mock humility deceived the
Jews, though probably not Lenin, who kept an eye
on him and used him.

Stalin was negligible and obtained one or two
negligible posts in the new government. As he was
a product of Georgian nationalism he was made
Commissar for Nationalities; he was later made
Inspector-General for Fields and Factories. These
posts were not necessarily sinecures, but Stalin
barely visited the respective offices once during the

first six months of their existence. Someone objected that these posts required an active and intelligent man. But Lenin laughed. "No intelligence is needed; that's why we've put Stalin there," said he.

Stalin was not discontented. An inexpert horseman does not wish to be given a wild horse. He was at least aware of his limitations. He is and always has been a watching man. He lay low and watched everybody. Most of all he watched Lenin, for he was a student of the technique of revolution. At his leisure he asked Lenin just what exactly he was supposed to do as Commissar of Nationalities. As a result of his consultations with the president a "Declaration of the Rights of Nationalities" was issued signed jointly. No one could denounce the declaration as heretical because, in any case, it bore Lenin's signature as well as his.

This document guaranteed freedom of religion and language and the right to set up if necessary a separate autonomous State. Unless we except the Finns, no national minority profited much by it, not even Georgia, but it was a useful counter-blast to the slogan of the Imperialists under Kornilof for a *Russia, One and Undivided*.

CHAPTER V

KORNILOF was a bullet-headed Siberian, brave and honourable but unintelligent. He was a capable soldier and a military leader who inspired confidence, but he lacked political sagacity. Although he figures now as a martyr of the revolution, it should be remembered that he had himself wished the revolution. The man who insulted the Tsaritsa on the day of her downfall could not obtain undivided allegiance from the counter-revolutionary elements in the army. It is true that numbers of officers who had gone home from the broken front for a long rest answered the call of civil war. But the Constitutionalists went to Kornilof and the Tsarists went to Denikin and Romanovsky. There was a division of loyalty in the White Army. Kornilof, menaced by the new Red Army, retreated from his headquarters at Rostof, on the Don, to the Caucasian Steppes.

Within two months of the arrival of Lenin in Petrograd, backed by mutinous sailors and the offscourings of the capital, the White forces a thousand miles away were in retreat. In November, Lenin was not even the master of the whole of Petrograd. He was entrenched in the Smolny Palace, which was defended by light artillery and machine guns and a numerous guard of soldiers and sailors, but the Provisional Government, although Kerensky had fled, was still nominally holding sessions in the Winter Palace. When the mob at last refused Prokopovitch, the acting prime minister, access to the Winter Palace, he and his colleagues

went over to the Town Hall to carry on the administration. The banks refused Lenin money but they
were raided. There was a great shortage of bread,
and foraging parties set off each day into the country
to rob the peasants. The headquarters of the Soviet
Government was a bandits' camp. And even within
that camp there was a great deal of discontent and
difference of opinion as to political strategy. Kamenef,
Zinovief and Trotsky at one point resigned and
decided to form a government of their own without
Lenin.

"Let's shoot them," said Stalin.

"No," said Lenin indifferently. "They'll come
running back."

Zinovief was the first to publish his repentance;
Trotsky, Rikof and Kamenef followed.

"People are either for us or against us," said
Lenin to Stalin.

"If they are against us they must be killed," said
Stalin.

"Well, there's something in that. We can only
win by terror."

The sailors made a beginning by murdering
Shingaref and Kokoshkin, two very respectable
ministers. Lenin refused to allow the murderers to
be seized by the police of the Provisional Government. Murders of less important people were not
only unpunished but almost unremarked. But
Lenin saw that murder must be legalised, and with
that in view he founded the Cheka, under the
presidency of that cold-blooded hater of Russians,
Felix Dzherzhinsky.

The remainder of the Provisional Government
was dispersed; the *Sovnarkom* assumed control and

wired the Commander-in-Chief of the Army to
approach the Germans and conclude an armistice
with a view to making an immediate peace. Dukhonin
replied that overtures for peace could only be
initiated by a responsible central government. To
that a further telegram was despatched: "In the
name of the Russian Republic, by the will of the
popular commissaries, you are removed from the
Command. . . . Ensign Krilenko is appointed
Commander - in - Chief. Signed, Lenin, Stalin,
Krilenko."

The rumour of armistice and peace spread like
wild-fire through Russia. It swayed millions to the
Red Flag. From the rapidly self-demobilising army
on the front were recruited the first units of the Red
Army. Trotsky was given the task of organising that
army. Stalin was content to be Lenin's crony and
batman. Lenin used him in a curious way. There
was a great disparity in intellectual outlook, yet
Lenin constantly sought Stalin's advice. He knew
that Stalin's will was much the same as his. They
could not disagree as regards policy. But Lenin was
not an autocrat. It gave him pleasure to say "Stalin
and I think. . . ." It must have annoyed Trotsky
when the latter telegraphed Lenin at Brest Litovsk
asking advice on a certain matter and Lenin replied: "Wait, I wish to confer with Stalin on that
point."

Stalin, in truth, did not look to be a formidable
competitor for power. He had no gift of speech
as Trotsky had. He was not an imposing figure.
He wore an old khaki tunic with a button missing.
It never went to the cleaners. His black hair was
uncouth; his thick moustache dropped. He did not

have his own automobile as Trotsky had. He was still smart at raiding banks and confiscating money for the Party, but money did not find its way into his pocket. He never showed off in any way. His face was a mask; it looked stupid and narrow-minded but benevolent. There was something of the mongrel terrier about him.

At the same time there was something underneath the ungainly exterior of Stalin which was soon to manifest itself. He possessed a most unexpected and unlikely gift for organisation. Under bourgeois institutions he might have run a department store in Tiflis with much success. In the first constructive months of Soviet rule his part was overshadowed by the genius of Lenin. Lenin had a flair for essentials of government and power. The elaboration of which Stalin was capable was not at the time required. The strategic positions in the political war had to be seized and Lenin saw to that. It was apart from Lenin, at the front in the Civil War, that Stalin first distinguished himself in a remarkable way.

Stalin saved Tsaritsin and the wheat. The defence of Tsaritsin against the Whites has been called in an exaggerated way the "Red Verdun." It was Stalin who organised it, and for that reason the city bears to-day the name of Stalingrad.

Kornilof had perished herocially and miserably in a campaign in which the casualties from exposure were almost as numerous as those from enemy fire, but in the spring of 1918 the Cossacks, under Drozdrof and Krasnof, rallied to fight more vigorously. Novocherkask, the historic centre of the Don Cossack country, was captured. Not only the

Northern Caucasus but the whole of the Don country almost to the Volga at Tsaritsin fell into the hands of the Whites. The food supply of the centre was threatened and Tsaritsin, as a key city for the shipment of grain, was most important to hold.

Tsaritsin was thought to be an objective of Kolchak and the Czech legions formed in Siberia; there was a distant danger of a united Siberian-Caucasian front. But the immediate danger was from the new-formed bands of counter-revolutionaries swarming north-eastward with capable and intrepid leaders. The Germans in occupation of the Ukraine were openly encouraging civil war.[1]

Voroshilof, a locksmith, was in command of the army for the relief of Tsaritsin, some 15,000 men, but Stalin went ahead of him with two armoured cars and a hundred or so Red guards. He found a city in which the old pre-war life had not disappeared. The cafés and taverns were open; there was music in the public gardens; there was dancing and promenading and light-hearted flirtation. The population was largely anti-Bolshevik, and was waiting in joyful anticipation to be captured by the Cossacks. The sympathies even of the garrison were in doubt. Men openly wore white favours in the streets. The Trade Unions were disaffected. The local Bolsheviks did not know whether it would be better to feign conversion to nationalism and so save their skins in case of a change of regime.

But in a very short while after the arrival of Stalin, invested with power of life and death and all other

[1] *Vide* Voroshilof, *Stalin and the Red Army* But perhaps they were not. It does not seem credible that the Germans had either ammunition or equipment to spare for the Cossacks, even if they favoured them, which is again doubtful. (S.G.)

possible Red authority, the city underwent a complete change. The cafés closed; the dancing stopped; the talkative population forebore to talk in the streets. The church bells ceased ringing. Armed sentries stood at the street-corners; plain-clothes men verified the papers of people who ventured out of doors. The city was changed to an armed camp with the strictest discipline. The Cheka was set up; the pale flag of terror was hoisted over Tsaritsin.

Within a fortnight the Whites had completely invested the city. Stalin was not daunted, but intensified his organisation of defence, keeping in close touch with Lenin, in Moscow, by wireless. Lenin approved of all that he did, but Trotsky, the president of the revolutionary war-council, had no part or lot in the defence. He seemed to overlook Tsaritsin as a war theatre of secondary importance, but he was in time to be annoyed by the success of Stalin.

"There were a lot of cobblers in charge of the army," wrote Stalin. The son of a cobbler used the word "cobbler" as a term of abuse. The uncouth Caucasian in a private's uniform was now military dictator of the Northern Caucasus. That was his style though all he commanded was Tsaritsin. But he bullied and drove the forces at his disposal like a Prussian martinet. His staff, composed of ex-officers of the Tsar's army and engineers, seemed to him either utterly incapable or indifferent as regards the issue of the struggle, for the most part poring over maps and indulging in pessimistic theories. But Stalin relieved them of their command and put men of his own choice in their places. Shells hurtled into the city day and night, a general attack by the enemy in force was momently expected, but the garrison held out till Voroshilof burst through with his fifteen thousand veterans.

Stalin then made Voroshilof commander, and together they consolidated the position. The danger of a rising within the city was now countered, and Stalin could deal more resolutely with the doubtful military personnel. There were many he would have had arrested earlier but it would not have been safe to arouse the disaffected population. Mass executions took place and almost the whole of the military staff sent to the city by Trotsky were placed under arrest and taken to a floating prison on the Volga. Trotsky telegraphed, "Set these men at liberty at once!" but Stalin countersigned the telegram: "No attention need be paid to this."

When Trotsky's men were ultimately released some of them went over to the enemy, notably Nosovitch, but after such treatment that is not surprising. However, they did not suit Stalin, who preferred to create a staff for the new Tenth Army out of younger, more enthusiastic human material. Here was Sergey Minin, who heroically repelled a raid of the Cossacks, a young student who wrote verses and eventually dramatised the siege of Tsaritsin in a play called *The City in the Ring*. He was the idol of the factory hands and the soldiers, and at one time could lead them to anything. Others, such as Valery Mezhlauk, were little more than boy scouts. Stalin found them and tested them then, but he has used them again since he has become dictator. They certainly made the defence a going concern. At the slightest sign of attack from without all the factory sirens howled the alarm. And such a chatter of machine guns and barking of rifle fire would ensue that the incapable Whites over-estimated the strength of the position.

Tsaritsin now was not entirely surrounded. One line of railway was working and the Volga was free. An evacuation could have been carried out in comparative safety. But Stalin and his young men intended to hold the city. They demanded and obtained rifles and ammunition from Trotsky though he complained bitterly that the Tsaritsin front was asking more than any other. As there were ammunition factories working in Tsaritsin it may be judged that the Tenth Army was really firing off a great deal.

Trotsky, safe at Moscow, became more and more irritated by Tsaritsin. His policy in creating the new Red Army was to staff it almost exclusively from the ex-officers of the old army. The policy of Stalin and Voroshilof was to consider such officers as unreliable and to staff the army from the young enthusiasts of the revolutionary movement. Trotsky, moreover, did not forgive the ignoring of his tele-gram. He went to Lenin and insisted upon Stalin's recall.

Meanwhile, at the beginning of August, General Krasnof made his most determined attack upon Tsaritsin. By one concentrated drive he was trying to force the Red units back across the Volga. Voro-shilof writes "For many days the Red troops, composed entirely of workers from the Donets Basin, withstood the extremely powerful attacks of the excellently organised Cossacks. These were great days of trial. You should have seen Comrade

Stalin at that time. Calm as usual, deep in thought, he literally had no sleep for days on end, distributing his intensive work between the fighting positions and the Army Headquarters. The position at the front became almost catastrophic. The Krasnof troops, commanded by Fitzhalaurof, Mamontof and others, by a well-planned manœuvre were pressing our exhausted troops who had already suffered great losses. The enemy front, formed into a horseshoe, with its flanks resting on the banks of the Volga, pressed closer to the city every day.

There was no way of escape but by the river. But Stalin was like one possessed, rallying the tired and desperate, lending the force of his will and personality to officers and men alike. And the Reds held on till the White energy had spent itself, then counter-attacked and drove the enemy in confusion back to the river Don.

The answer to that was Stalin was recalled. Trotsky must have said to Lenin, "It is either he or I, one of us must go." Lenin was diplomatic; he could not afford to lose Trotsky. His own position was none too sound. Even in Moscow itself there had been an armed insurrection against him. The intrepid Savinkof, the greatest terrorist and assassin of the revolutionary movement, was with the disgruntled Social Revolutionary party working for Lenin's destruction. Trotsky was nearer them in political belief than he was to the Bolsheviks. "We can't have any quarrelling," said Lenin. "If you want it, Stalin shall be recalled."

Sverdlof was sent express to Stalin to persuade him to give up. As it happened that suited Stalin very well. The task which he had set himself was accomplished. The city was now out of immediate danger unless very much larger forces were brought to bear upon it. All burghers whose sympathies were uncertain had either been imprisoned or shot. The Tenth Army was in good shape and the ammunition factories were working well. Grain and food supplies were moving steadily north to the provisioning of Moscow and the centre. Stalin was quite ready to move to another region of the widespread revolutionary field.

At the same time, it may be doubted whether he would have flouted the authority of Lenin. Trotsky, even then, he did not respect, but Lenin was his master, not to say his god. On his way back he met Trotsky, who in all his grandeur as war chief was visiting Tsaritsin in the Imperial train, for all the world like a Tsar. He greeted Stalin *de haut en bas*, "Ah, here we have the Caucasian cockroach, let me get into a good position where I can see this little man!"

Stalin, in his dirty yellow tunic and tousled hair, gave himself no airs. He was pleased to see the "great Trotsky." Trotsky made him a speech to which he listened with apparent humility and modesty. He must have confirmed Trotsky in the belief that he was really stupid and negligible. But actually Stalin was afraid that Trotsky would make a clean sweep of his Tsaritsin organisation and in effect deliver the place over to the enemy.

"I hope you won't chase them out," said Stalin. "They're fine lads."

"Ho," said Trotsky. "Those fine lads of yours are destroying the revolution. I go to do one thing: to bring Tsaritsin within the Soviet Republic."

Stalin grimaced and smiled. It was not his moment to argue with Trotsky. The time was to come when Stalin would give his answer. Now his strongest move was to go to Lenin. That fact in itself must enjoin some caution in Trotsky's actions.

CHAPTER VI

THE affairs of Lenin were not very promising in the autumn of 1918. France and England, under cover of the great conflict with Germany, were committing themselves to a war with Red Russia. There was no declaration of war, but cynical politicians took the easier way of pretending that Russian intervention was a protective measure against Germany. And the Censorship, ostensibly employed to hide the truth from the Germans, provided a useful means to hide the Russian adventure from the working class populations of France and England.

France and England had tacitly entered the field for Kerensky or at least for a constitutional State on Western lines capable of protecting the commercial and financial privileges of the two countries. In short they fought for bonds and oil, certainly not for Tsarism or Russia. The political aspect of this intervention was distasteful to the Russian monarchists but the intervention was a great menace to the Bolsheviks and but for the Armistice might have proved successful.

Throughout the war on the Eastern front great numbers of Czechs and Slovaks had surrendered out of the Austrian army without fighting. These Slavs hated the Austrian power and had marched over to the Russian lines in whole battalions, singing. They went to Siberia with the rest of the German prisoners, but when the Bolsheviks made peace with Germany there was a danger that they might be repatriated

with the rest of the German prisoners to be re-drafted
into the Austrian army or to be shot for treason.
Naturally they were not very anxious to go home on
those terms.

The Czech legions partially armed by Kerensky
under the influence of Masaryk, who was in Russia
from May, 1917, to April, 1918, became greatly
increased after the peace of Brest Litovsk. They
trailed in trains all the way from the Urals to Vladi-
vostok. In May, 1918, the Bolsheviks demanded the
surrender of their arms, and some who were in
danger of capture by the Reds did surrender them.
But their numbers were augmented by the adherence
of Russian officers. Instead of the legionnaires being
transhipped to Europe to fight on the Western front
they were converted into an anti-Bolshevik army.
A White hope was born in Siberia. A Russian White
Army appeared as from nowhere and bands of
volunteers and ex-officers seized the great cities of
Siberia, Omsk and Irkutsk and Cheliabinsk on the
Ural border, pulled down the red flags, chased
out the commissars, seized all arms and ammunition and of course whatever gold they could lay
hands on.

The Czech Legion turning their arms westward
entered city after city as on parade without firing a
shot. By August they had actually taken Kazan,
the great city on the Volga. That corresponded to
the time when Stalin was recalled and Trotsky took
over the defence of Tsaritsin. The Whites of the
Caucasus and the Don took immense encouragement
from the fact that the whole of Siberia seemed freed
from Bolshevism. They attacked the Red Armies
in the South with new *élan* and aided by an insurgent

peasantry tired of being robbed of their grain they began to advance toward the centre.

Stalin having given Lenin his version of the state of affairs at Tsaritsin asked to be sent to help organise the Southern front, which at that time seemed the most threatening. Trotsky did not wish to have him on the war staff on any terms. Lenin, however, was impressed by Stalin's achievement and did not penetrate Stalin's mock humility when he said: "I am quite willing to work under Trotsky's direction if I can go on with what I have been doing."

Lenin was a firm believer in *esprit de corps* and encouraged no quarrels. He wrote to Trotsky telling him fairly all that Stalin had reported about Tsaritsin, including a statement that the city had nearly been lost owing to the parsimony of the war department in sending ammunition. Finally he declared that Trotsky must accommodate himself to Stalin's ideas and co-operate with him. The letter was couched in such terms that it was difficult for Trotsky to take a strong line. Somewhat weakly, it must be said, Trotsky agreed and allowed Stalin to join the war staff on the Southern front. That was an error if Trotsky firmly believed that it was fatal to allow young communists to run the army rather than ex-officers of the Tsar's army.

In any case, he proceeded to get rid of all Stalin's "heroes" in Tsaritsin. In December he demanded of Lenin that Voroshilof be relieved as he could not work with him. And with Voroshilof the rest of the staff was dismissed and Trotsky had a new staff of his own choosing and a new commander.

Voroshilof and the rest joined Stalin at Kharkhof which suited the Georgian very well. But affairs in

the South were in a parlous condition. Trotsky's
army down there showed itself quite incapable.
Stalin arrived too late to organise any point of resistance. Vast areas of grain land and supplies fell into
the hands of the Whites. And General Wrangel
took Tsaritsin. That chapter was closed.

Trotsky was ready to blame Stalin for the débâcle
on the Southern front. He demanded from Lenin
the complete dismissal from the army of Stalin and
Voroshilof. "I consider the protection by Stalin
of the Tsaritsin movement in the army a most dangerous disease," he wrote. "Stalin, Voroshilof and
Co. mean catastrophe for us all."

"We must compromise on that," wired Lenin,
always desirous of smoothing matters over.

Trotsky was obstinate, and Lenin might have
recalled Stalin from the Southern front as he did
previously from Tsaritsin. But Stalin had taken
himself off. Probably he thought the Southern
imbroglio too much for him. He went to the Eastern
front to face Kolchak and the Siberian army.

CHAPTER VII

To appease Trotsky Lenin had decided that Stalin be sent to the Eastern front to enquire into the question of drunkenness in the army. Kolchak's army had invaded European Russia and taken Perm. The Third Army had fled in confusion, losing 18,000 men and a vast number of guns, especially machine guns, abandoning stores, ammunition and transport. Trotsky's pet ex-officers had deserted *en masse* to the side where their true sympathies lay. Stalin's real mission was to find out what exactly led to the fall of Perm and to reorganise a base for military operations.

Lenin telegraphed Trotsky: "We have despatches from Perm relating to drunkenness in the army and its broken morale. I propose sending Stalin as I am afraid Smilga would not be firm enough." To this Trotsky agreed.

It was then decided by the central committee of the Soviet that Dzherzhinsky and Stalin be sent "to examine minutely the cause of the surrender of Perm and of the recent defeats on the Ural front and to take all measures for the restoration of political and military discipline."

And so, although going ostensibly to close up vodka shops and patch up discipline, Stalin was in reality setting off to perform the same service to the Soviet as when he went to Tsaritsin the year before. On January 5th, 1919, he telegraphed to Lenin as follows:—

"The investigation is proceeding and we hope to inform you as to its progress. At the moment there is one thing especially urgent. Of the 30,000 originally composing the Third Army there remain only 11,000 worn out men who are almost incapable of resistance to the enemy's attacks. The reinforcements sent by Trotsky did not prove reliable. Some of the recruits sent us are disaffected. If we are to save Viatka, which is now in great danger, three absolutely reliable regiments should be sent up at once. We urge you to bring immediate pressure upon the authorities concerned. Otherwise what happened at Perm will be repeated at Viatka. This is the common opinion of the comrades here and is shared by us having regard to all the information available.

Signed:—STALIN, DZHERZHINSKY.

5th *January*, 1919, *Viatka*."

Stalin understood his work as military re-organisation. Dzherzhinsky went on with his congenial occupation of inquisition and torture. The local Cheka at Viatka was re-staffed with sterner men. There was short shrift for doubtful comrades at Viatka.

In answer to the telegram 1,200 picked men and two squadrons of cavalry were at once despatched to Viatka. And another regiment which had been verified as to its political morale also arrived before the end of the month. These reinforcements were scanty but actually proved adequate for the defence of the city. The Whites only needed to be met with disciplined resistance to prove that they also were poor fighting material.

Since the Armistice in November, 1918, the Czechs had done little to help the Russians and the allied missions in Siberia. Now that the Great War was over and they could not be called upon to fight for the Germans they were eager to get home. Moreover, their nation had constituted itself as the new republic of Czecho-Slovakia. It was natural that their hearts should not be in this alien struggle in Siberia. Kolchak was a fine character but greatly thwarted by those who were supposed to be helping him.

Not only was the White offensive arrested in front of Viatka but to the East the Red Army began a successful flanking movement and the city of Uralsk was retaken. In the month of his arrival on the Eastern front things took a turn for the better. The Whites outnumbered the Reds, and in January, 1919, could no doubt, have penetrated far into European Russia spreading disaffection and disorganisation as they went but they let go by their best moment. The Czech commander remained in masterly inactivity at Perm dreaming of joining up with the British forces advancing from Archangel. No doubt he intended to advance when the Red Army should have melted away in front of him. But it did not melt. Stalin, the man of steel, was there seeing to it that it did not melt.

Felix Dzhérzhinsky played his part in this arena. The new Cheka at Viatka extended its activity. The Communist inquisition combed out the Ural border. Terror hushed the chattering populations. The Pole was cruel; he was more than that, he was insensate. It is commonly thought that cruelty is a bad ally for any cause. But that has not been proved in the Russian revolution. The crueller side won.

This may be due to the fact that the Slavs are passive towards suffering. There is sympathy for the intellectual sufferings of others but there is not much sympathy for physical suffering. On hearing of other people's sufferings the Russian asks God for mercy. He does not rush to arms. The saying of Tacitus with regard to the leader of a punitive expedition—"He made a desert and called it peace," has often been applied in Russia. A sad fact about Russia is that cruelty has usually paid the practisers of it. Dzherzhinsky did sound work for the central government of Moscow and he is worthy of his monument.

Stalin, without sharing the Pole's ferocity, made a friend of Dzherzhinsky at Viatka. In colloquial terms Stalin and Dzherzhinsky were "thick as thieves." It was rather more than mutual help and co-operation which bound them. Stalin was resolute to "clean up" the Siberian front; Dzherzhinsky was ready to do the cleaning. But there was something else. Stalin, as with Lenin, was learning something which could further him in his political career. A front, a group of people, a population could be be brought under his complete personal control by the determined exclusion of all doubtful elements and the elimination of heresy. Later, in the Communist party itself, in Moscow, he was going to "filter" in the same way as he had "filtered" at Viatka.

Also he retained Dzherzhinsky as an ally in the coming struggle for power. Dzherzhinsky, as a Pole, naturally hated Russians, and he was not warm towards the Jews. An association with a Georgian was not intolerable to him and he felt that Stalin must naturally share his own antipathies. In the latter surmise he was wrong, for Stalin has no racial prejudices. Only he is clever enough to seem to share other men's prejudices when it is advantageous to do so.

Stalin and Dzherzhinsky were, however, alike in that they were both militant communists. Lenin was only tacitly so. He had studied British political methods with some admiration of technique, and had assimilated the method of compromise and of "divide and rule." Stalin by himself would not have compromised the revolution to such an extent as Lenin ultimately did by the New Economic Policy. His instinctive primitive way was that of destruction and elimination. Whoever stood in the way of the revolution should be shot. Dzherzhinsky agreed, but at the same time preferred to use more cruelty in dealing with prisoners. Dzherzhinsky was the embodiment of the Terror and the most feared man in the whole regime.

The friendship with him served Stalin in another way. It was dangerous to thwart Stalin when he had all the while the ear of the Cheka and could have whom he liked put to the question.

Trotsky's enmity toward Stalin became therefore isolated. It was a one-man enmity and could not cause Stalin much trouble, the more especially as Trotsky himself, as head of the war department, was not covering himself with glory.

The Soviet Republic was hard-pressed in the spring and summer of 1919. Kolchak held Siberia; Denikin was advancing from the South; British warships stood in the Gulf of Finland; a mixed army of Russians, Esthonians, British, under General Judenitch, was within sight of Petrograd. The British were threatening to advance from their base at Archangel at the melting of the snows.

Trotsky made speeches which were so violent one could see he was frightened. Defeat, capture and death began to menace the Soviet leaders. Lenin however, kept calm. He did not indulge in the histrionics of Trotsky but instead called Stalin to the rescue, to put things right at the chief point of danger—Petrograd.

What he had accomplished at Tsaritsin and Viatka he was asked to repeat at Kronstadt and Petrograd. There was mutiny, disaffection, desertion, panic. Whole regiments were going over to the Whites. The garrisons of two of the forts of Kronstadt had opened fire on the Reds.

Stalin was again at the point of the greatest danger. Petrograd was rife with counter-revolutionary conspiracy and at the same time there was a White Army advancing upon it. This time Stalin had with him, not Dzherzhinsky but another ruthless character, the notorious Peters. It seemed almost certain that the city would capitulate to the national forces and more than half the population was quietly burning its red flags and preparing some joyful morning to hang out the double eagle again. Some were not too quiet in their preparations and openly boasted that they had always been against the revolution. Those who had established themselves in the luxurious apartments and mansions abandoned by the wealthy changed into custodians over night. The revengeful prepared lists of their neighbours for execution. Others were furtively digging holes outside the city to hide their stolen gold. Apparently no one believed that the advance of Judenitch could be stemmed.

But there was a fateful delay and hesitancy in the counsels of Judenitch. He was not a capable soldier and his army was not reliable. He gave the enemy a breathing space for reorganisation. Stalin proceeded at once to mobilise a new Red Army from the workers in the Putilof factories and other industrial plants, and from all the more trusty young Communists he could find. It was an army made of odds and ends.

"Pallid, scowling, with shadowy, starved faces, narrow-shouldered, clumsy, in long trousers and old boots done up with string, carrying sacks and cartridges tied together with string, with Austrian rifles on their shoulders pointing at all angles, this army in a drab mass rolled along the streets, smoking cigarettes. They did not look like soldiers. They were not the healthy Russian infantry we all know, but smelt of bad tobacco and sweat," says General Krasnof.

And this armed rabble, aided by armoured cars, sallied forth from Peter the Great's city and put the fear of God into the Whites. Add an armoured train slowly making toward Tsarskoe Selo and belching fire as it went.

The White Army retired to reorganise and await reinforcements from Great Britain. The forts at Kronstadt were recaptured by the Reds. Stalin was able to wire Lenin:—"The hostile warships have not engaged us being evidently afraid of the re-established forts. . . . Deserters are returning to us in thousands. . . . The Whites are in flight."

The failure of Judenitch to capture the city in the spring gave the Cheka its opportunity of revenge in the summer, and those who had rashly announced their anti-revolutionary sympathies felt the red hand of Peters. The name of Petrograd was later changed to Leningrad which was an insult of a kind. It remained disaffected despite the cleansing efforts of the Cheka. It was still disaffected when Judenitch returned to the attack in the autumn. Stalin has never been popular there, and it might have become a base for a new revolutionary movement led by Trotsky or Zinovief had those two leaders had the courage and capacity to avail themselves of it.

CHAPTER VIII

THEN Stalin was switched to the Southern front which in turn became the most menacing to the Soviet Republic. Denikin had taken Kursk and Orel. Tula was threatened. The central agricultural region round about Moscow was being raided by Cossack bands. The initiative was with the Whites. The bewildered Bolsheviks never seemed to be able to establish defensive lines on the vast terrain of the conflict. Nevertheless Denikin's forces were over-extended. Many of the advance parties were acting independently and were not in close touch with the commander and showed more energy in looting than in fighting. Trotsky's plan of making a flank attack from the Southern Volga near Tsaritsin might have met with success if carried out with a sufficient number of men. It had, however, the disadvantage of being anticipated and expected by Denikin and might conceivably have been met by the main body of the White Army under a very capable soldier, Wrangel. Stalin would not countenance Trotsky's strategy on any terms.

The rising importance and prestige of Stalin may be understood by the fact that before accepting the invitation of the revolutionary council to go to the Southern front he stipulated that Trotsky should not be allowed to interfere in any way with the campaign there. He also obtained permission to retire the officers of Trotsky's choice and replace them with men of his own choosing. This was the first great rebuff to Trotsky in the revolution and he received it at the hands of Stalin.

The Soviet gave Stalin *carte blanche*. Trotsky's plan of campaign was shelved. Stalin took matters into his own hands, being nevertheless careful to keep in personal touch with Lenin by telegraph, informing him of his proposed changes and his plan of action. He poured scorn on Trotsky's pet idea of an attack over the Steppes, calling it stupidity and obstinacy . . . "what does this cockerel know of strategy?" An advance through Cossack country could have but one effect, that of rousing the whole Cossack population to fury.

The new plan of campaign was for an advance through the centre toward Little Russia with Kharkhov as an objective, thence to threaten Rostof on the Don. "Here," he wrote Lenin, "we would find ourselves among a friendly and not a hostile population which must facilitate our advance. We should find ourselves in possession of an important railway artery and cut the line Voronezh-Rostof which has been vital for Denikin's supplies. We outflank the Cossacks and threaten them from the rear. If we are successful in our advance Denikin will most probably wish to reinforce his centre with Cossacks which they will not want to do, and we could count on that breeding trouble among the Whites. Then we should get supplies of coal (from the Donets basin) and Denikin would be deprived of coal."

Stalin urged Lenin to approve this plan of attack as the only one promising success, declaring that his presence on the Southern front would be waste of time, "futile, criminal, useless" if the plan were over-ridden, and that he would in that case rather go to the devil than remain there.

On this Voroshilof comments: "The road from Tsaritsin to Novorossisk might have turned out to be much longer because it went through an environment of class enemies. On the other hand the way from Tula to Novorossisk might prove much shorter because it went through working-class Kharkhov and the mining region of the Donets Basin. In Stalin's estimation of the correct line of attack can be seen his chief quality as a proletarian revolutionary, the real strategist of the Civil War."

Voroshilof was a bosom friend of Stalin's. It is true the plan succeeded. Trotsky took over the defence of Petrograd and was busily employed but in fairness it may be urged that there is no proof that Trotsky's strategy on the Southern front would not have proved as successful ultimately as that of Stalin. The germ of failure was in the brain of Denikin who was not capable of controlling the immense forces at his disposal at the time.

Lenin signed the order for the cancellation of Trotsky's instructions and the Central Soviet advised Stalin to go ahead. His judgment was at once confirmed by success. At the first serious attack the White Army of the centre recoiled and the widespread guerrilla bands in danger of being isolated and destroyed fled precipitately, infecting the whole army with their panic.

Not the least important advantage of the initial victory was the capture of a great number of undamaged rifles and abundant ammunition. There were food supplies not only for the army but for Moscow. Many horses were also taken. Stalin chose the moment to develop a favourite idea, the formation of a cavalry army. In open warfare such as that in which they were engaged any advantage obtained could not be pushed without vigorous and numerous cavalry. The Red Cossacks contributed greatly to the discomfiture of Denikin's army. Budenny, their commander, became a household name and children's hero in Soviet Russia.

Denikin was routed and fled to the sea. The great Southern fighting force of the Whites was destroyed and though out of its ruin emerged the puny, bedraggled army of General Wrangel occupying the Crimea, the menace to the Soviet State was definitely lifted. Much the same fate had overtaken Kolchak's army in Siberia, and Kolchak himself had been handed over by the unsympathetic Czechs to be butchered by the Red soldiery. Trotsky with his armoured trains had finally disposed of Judenitch. The last card in the counter-revolutionary game was played by Poland aided by France in the late summer of 1920 and that failed also, although Polish arms met with some success. Then Wrangel could not face the massed machine guns of the Reds and hurried off with his staff and what the British could save of his army, and took refuge in Constantinople.

Too much stress might be put upon the glory of the Bolshevik victories. The proletarian army fought well and it was at times capably handled, but it is truer to say that the Whites lost than that the Reds won. The Whites ought to have won, but they were not of one mind politically. They did not know whether they were fighting for a constitutional republic or for Tsarism, for a throne for the Grand Duke Nicholas or for a throne for the legitimate heir, the Grand Duke Cyril, or for a presidency for Professor Milyukof. Their counsels were confused by the presence of British and French agents who were fundamentally more interested in commercial concessions than in Russia herself, and were obviously working for some sort of subservient government that would fulfil the commercial and financial programme they had in view. There was also great corruption and embezzlement at the bases of the armies. The story of the counter-revolutionary movement is pitiful.

CHAPTER IX

THEY had been fighting to decide whether Russia should be a Marxist republic or a national State. The partisans of Marxism won but when they had won they found that Marxism was impracticable. When the bourgeois had been destroyed they bid the bourgeois rise from the dead. Lenin made the enigmatic remark: "We may sometimes add two and two and say it is five but we do not say it is a tallow candle." Marxism was coming indubitably, but it was necessary to pronounce some magic word first. Lenin tried to find the word. He tried the word "Electrificatsia." The word had a great boom; everybody in Russia said it, though several million were doubtful as to its meaning. Mothers called their children "Electrificatsia," being now free to go outside the book of saints for names. All Russia was to be electrified as a preparation for the new era. The word failed and has almost been forgotten. Stalin was as usual attentive. The word was wrong, but perhaps the idea underlying it was right. That idea was "mechanisation." In due course Stalin found another word; that word was "Tractor."

But that is to anticipate history. First Lenin introduced the "New Economic Policy" which legalised money again and allowed shops to open, invited foreign capital, made possible commercial concessions to foreign companies. Making war on Capitalism they invited the co-operation of capitalists.

Stalin, though subservient to his master and idol, was not sympathetic to the change. Militant communism suited his temperament better. He was a primitive Caucasian with the blood of bandits in his veins and on his hands. At that time the best way to get bread for the towns as he understood it was to raid the peasantry. Lenin defined militant communism as "grabbing the peasants' grain for the army." But another writer gives it a fuller characterisation:—"The only thing not controlled by the State was love. Without an order from the Soviet you could not hire a lodging. You must be in the State service to obtain a food ticket. Without a permit you were not allowed to travel on the railway. Every house, every room was supervised by the Cheka. Son denounced father, father son, wife husband, just to get a bit of bread. The shops were closed; the State depots of goods were almost empty. Goods stolen from the government supplies were sold in secret cellars and basements and barns. The Cheka routing out the miscreants, arrested, banished, shot. The most terrible terror reigned in the land.[1]

But the important point about this regime was not its ferocity but that it did not work. Even the most trusty Reds were at times short of boots and rations. And obviously no system could last based on the widespread ill-will of the masses of the people.

In March, 1921, the Communist Party was holding its tenth congress. At the same time, like a new disruptive movement, there broke out a proletarian insurrection in Kronstadt. Not Whites this time, but Reds were in rebellion. Soldiers and sailors and

[1] S. Dmitrievsky: *Stalin*, pp. 245-6.

factory workers demanded the exclusion of the
Communist party from the control of the country.

"Free Soviets! Free Business! Down with the
Communists!" were their slogans.

Stalin was given the congenial task of "cleaning
up" Kronstadt. Trotsky was sent first, but got into
a bad state of nerves. It is possible that he was
vaguely aware of a chance for himself to lead a new
movement. He had always been more in favour of
Evolutionary Socialism than of Communism. Kronstadt was actually proceeding to the task of forming
a new revolutionary government and had the insurrection spread like wild fire throughout Russia it is
possible that Lenin might have been displaced and
Trotsky have become ruler. In any case he took
no firm action. Stalin and Voroshilof were sent
after him and took matters into their own hands.
Trotsky remained nominally head of the punitive
expedition but Stalin organised it and did the work.

Troops and artillery were hurried to the siege of
Kronstadt. Field guns on sleighs were somehow
transported on the melting and breaking ice to
sea-ward of the city. The fortress was mercilessly
shelled, the idea being to drive the inhabitants out
like rats. Their escape out of Russia by the sea was
barred. "None shall escape our revenge," said
Stalin.

The recalcitrant Red fortress was taken and a
medieval slaughter of the inhabitants ensued. For
a week thousands of bullets, spluttered with blood
into the walls and mortar of Kronstadt. Not only
were the mutinous Reds shot but many of the
Communists who had been imprisoned by them.
They ought not to have allowed themselves to be

imprisoned, and therefore they were executed with
the rest. The mutineers demanding free shopkeeping
were no doubt right but they paid for having thought
of it first. Lenin took their signal and made a
compromise. The "New Economic Policy" was
introduced.

"Continued prohibition of trading and property
owning is tantamount to suicide for the Communist
party," said he. "We must remedy our mistakes."

Among the Reds only Lenin had the authority
and prestige to be able to make such a *volte-face*.
It was deeply distasteful to the young Communists
and to what may be called the heroes of Tsaritsin,
and to Stalin himself. But Stalin understood that
if Lenin wanted the new policy he would make it.
Stalin estimated the forces in the political field
and decided to lie low and hide his discontent.

So all the petty traders were allowed to come out
into the open, and as if by magic Moscow changed
overnight into a cheap fair and old-clothes market.
The whole population, deprived for so long of their
favourite occupation, started buying and selling and
buying again. The turn-over of the clever dealers
was rapid. Commercial civilisation as we know it
started again for nothing, rapidly producing richer
and poorer, in short putting men and women into
classes again.

The new birth of bourgeois society was naturally
abhorrent to those who had fathered it. Some
chastening, almost a change of mind about it was
inevitable. The more successful shopkeepers soon
received the attention of the Cheka, were arrested,
imprisoned, sent to death on Solovetsky and else-
where. But the N.E.P. was not abrogated, and new

nepmen took the places of those whom the Cheka removed.

Stalin, with the facility of a parrot, repeated what Lenin said. "Can the Communist Party impose its leadership on the people by force? No, it cannot. If such a thing were done the leadership would not last long."

Zinovief was strongly opposed to the N.E.P. and doubted Lenin's judgment. "It is a retreat and nothing more," said he.

"No," said Stalin. "It is only at the outset that the N.E.P. can be looked upon as a retreat. It is so designed that in the course of this initial retreat we may be able to regroup our forces and resume the offensive."

One of the main objects of the N.E.P. commonly overlooked in the bewildering spectacle of city trading was the re-establishment of the agricultural community, whose life had not only become intolerable but senseless owing to State robbery. The peasants sowed less and less because their harvests were stolen from them. If persecuted further by marauding bands the peasantry had the power in their hands to starve out the whole of the rest of the nation. Socialising the peasantry by rude force had already proved a failure. It was necessary to find some more practical mode of compulsion. Stalin's peace with the N.E.P. may be expressed in the words of Lenin: "Out of the Russia of the New Economic Policy shall arise a socialist Russia." It was Stalin's view that the position of the peasant should be stabilised temporarily by the N.E.P. and then when a new method was found they should go to the country again and socialise it.

Trotsky, however, interpreted the compromise of the N.E.P. to mean that a full complete proletarian revolution could only be accomplished in Russia after world revolution. Russia must wait on the West. "The real growth of the Socialist economy in Russia can take place only after the victory of the proletariat in the more important countries of Europe." Trotsky was nearer to Lenin's international outlook at that time. Lenin still warmly entertained the thought of general European revolution, but Stalin's gaze was riveted upon Russia, probably also upon his own career. Russians in general knew little about Europe and cared less, and Stalin was like them in that. "Russia first: Europe afterwards," epitomises his view.

After Lenin's death the development of the N.E.P. proved naturally a matter of considerable dispute. It became a testing stone for the genuineness of revolutionary opinions. It had compromised Lenin's position as a good Communist. It was a practical admission that pure Communism would not work and was such an outrage on the life of the individual that it must result in social chaos and counter-revolution. That in Lenin's purpose it was to lead in course of time to stricter Communism is doubtful. It was a compromise which led logically to the establishment of a commercial republic.

But whatever it was intended to be, it has not proved easy to get rid of it. And the interpretation of what Lenin meant by it has ruined the career of many Russian politicians.

CHAPTER X

BOTH Lenin and Stalin began to be troubled by symptoms of physical ill health. Both felt the strain which the incessant work and anxiety of the revolution had placed upon them. Since the death of Sverdlof (March, 1919) Lenin had been over-burdened with work. Sverdlof acted as secretary and intermediary for Lenin, taking off his hands an enormous amount of routine labour. Lenin was no man of steel like Stalin but a nervous, pot-bellied man with impure blood. Periods of brilliant intellectual vision and free use of undivided will alternated with periods of apathy and weakness.

Stalin, who in war time lived on bread and salt, onions, garlic, red wine, was menaced by abdominal trouble. He had pain after eating, followed by enforced abstinence and consequent weakness. The trouble was, however, intermittent. After nursing himself for a while the pain and weakness would disappear and he found himself as fit and energetic as before. He had a severe attack of pain after the campaign against Denikin, and was obliged to rest and do nothing. Lenin wished him to follow up his successes and deal with Wrangel as he had dealt with Denikin, but he made various excuses such as "the local party organisations may think me frivolous, jumping from one sphere of activity to another." The Central Committee, however, ordered him to go. He went therefore to organise the new front but broke down and was unable to continue. That was in September, 1920. In the winter he recovered

and proved well enough to deal energetically with
the insurrection at Kronstadt when he was sent to
quell it. But after that he fell seriously ill once
more and even seemed to be threatened with death.
Though loth to consult doctors or other skilled
members of the bourgeois class he was bound now
to seek expert medical aid if he wished to survive.

Doctor Rozanof, to whom he had recourse, diag-
nosed an acute attack of appendicitis. There were
complications; a considerable amount of bowel had
to be cut away. Stalin was operated upon in the
Soldatenkovsky Hospital, in Moscow. The operation
did not appear to be entirely successful. It had,
perhaps, been delayed too long. For some days the
patient hovered between life and death.

This illness touched a soft spot in Lenin. Those
threatened by death are more sympathetic toward
the dying than those possessed of robust health.
Lenin had been surprised by the capacity and energy
of the humble Stalin. He heartily disliked Stalin's feud
with Trotsky and was afraid of it. He had penetrated
the psychology of Stalin and began to see his over-
weening ambition. It had undoubtedly occurred to
him while Stalin was in good health: Stalin is going
to be dangerous. But Stalin dying was different.
Then he remembered that Stalin was the one
Bolshevik who had never swerved in loyalty to
himself, the man who had believed in him more
fervently than any other. Stalin was his protégé,
the man he had protected from intrigue, the man
whose hidden intelligence and ability he had himself
spotted when others had called him a Caucasian
monkey. He therefore was a constant visitor at the
hospital during the critical days of Stalin's illness

and when at last he learned that he was out of danger, he thanked the doctor effusively for his care.

Rozanof recommended that his patient be moved as early as possible to his native Georgia for convalescence. "Yes," said Lenin. "That's a good idea, somewhere far away from Moscow where there will be no one to bother him."

This was Trotsky's hour of glory. Now that the Whites had been dispersed on every front, for which he took most of the credit, he comported himself with royal state, rode his white horse on parade, drove in the Tsar's automobile with guards on the step, lived in sumptuous apartments. Out of Russia his fame was even greater than within. He was second only to Lenin and was regarded as the natural inheritor of his power. The army seriously believed he was a great soldier and the envious whispered that he dreamed of becoming a second Napoleon. The history of the French revolution has proved an untrustworthy guide as to the development of the revolution in Russia.

Becoming a Napoleon must have been far from Trotsky's thoughts, but undoubtedly he did believe that in due course he would become the controller of the revolution. He was the second in command and he had no serious rival. Neither Zinovief nor Kamenef were sure of themselves. They had been excitable timorous wobblers from the first and intellectually Trotsky was their superior. Also though he disagreed with the president on many matters he had the ear and confidence of Lenin and he was on good terms with Lenin's wife, Krupskaya, who preferred his influence to that of Stalin.

The first *Politbureau*, the equivalent of a cabinet

in Western parlance, was composed of Lenin, Trotsky, Stalin and Kamenef. The secretaries of the central committee of the Communist Party were Krestinsky, Serebriakof and Stasof, who were in the nature of clerks and had no political initiative or influence. Lenin, in a sense, was above the Party and above the government. In 1922 the control of the Party over the government was not complete. It is possible that had Trotsky got into the saddle he would have divorced the government from the Communist Party and made it elective and responsible to an electorate purely and simply. The *Sovnarkom* would then have had undivided authority. The apparatus of the Party for controlling the government was not perfected at that time. The triple secretariat had no directing force. Lenin told the Party what it should do and it did it. The Party in fact cloaked the autocracy of Lenin as the will of the revolution. In essence the dictatorship of the Party meant— "We, the leaders, are going to have what we want, not what the proletariat of Russia may think they want."

Lenin felt the need of a strong man in the secretariat of the Party, someone who could organise it and control it and settle out of hand a hundred and one small matters that were being referred to him. He had not the strength to cope with all the business of the Party. The shadow of illness was over Lenin and he alone knew it. He began to be seriously concerned as to the future of the revolution. The post of secretary to the Communist Party was one which, while seeming modest enough at the time, might become exceedingly important after his death. Stalin had offered himself for the post but Lenin, who knew the concealed strength .and oriental craftiness of the Georgian, feared at first to give it him.

There was, however, no intrigue to get the post. Trotsky did not want it. He must have overlooked its significance. As for Stalin, although he had thwarted him in the war, Trotsky still under-rated his intelligence. He thought that Stalin was a rather stupid aboriginal from the Caucasus, a merciless barbarian who had been useful in extirpating the enemies of the revolution, now tolerated in power by the friendly loyalty of Lenin. The war finished, there was nothing for a Georgian to do. Naturally he fell ill. Stalin, the sick man, virtually banished to the Caucasus, did not disturb the ambitious vision of Comrade Trotsky.

But Stalin recovered and returned. Lenin, against his better judgment, decided to make him secretary of the Party. Lenin was getting weaker; perhaps he was overborne by a will that was stronger than his own.

He told Trotsky of his decision.

"The new cook will prepare us some peppery dishes," said Lenin.

Trotsky shrugged his shoulders.

In the spring of 1922 the appointment was made and Stalin set to work at once to gather the whole power of the Communist Party into his own hands. Lenin watched him with misgiving, but his strength of personality was failing him. Instead of bearding him in the office of the Party and turning him out, he wrote his opinions weakly on a tablet. "Comrade Stalin," he wrote, "having become general secretary, has concentrated enormous power in his hands, and I am not sure that he knows how to use that power with sufficient caution. . . . He is too rough, and this fault, entirely supportable in relations among us Communists, becomes insupportable in the office of secretary, and I propose to the comrades to find a way to remove Stalin from his position. . ."

But Lenin was ill. In May, 1922, he had a stroke and lost the use of his right arm and left leg. He was threatened with general paralysis. His enemies said he had venereal or tabes; his friends called it degeneration of the spinal tissues. The doctors did not hold out much hope for him. The disease would extend and even if he did not die speedily he must be rendered quite helpless.

CHAPTER XI

"WE will now forget past differences and be friends and work together," said Stalin to Trotsky. Stalin approached him with a sort of easy familiarity. But Trotsky was aloof. "For every step forward I took a step backward and passed by," he wrote.

Lenin had been the unifying factor of the Communist Party but with Lenin sick it was divided by faction. Kamenef had his adherents as had Zinovief. Trotsky had filled all the principal offices with his own men. The adherents of Stalin were among the younger and more obscure members. It was necessary for him to seek alliances and set one faction against another. Trotsky would not lend himself to the intrigue, so he set to work to win to his side another faction. At the same time he began a careful revision of the membership of the Party.

Now the *Politbureau* of which Stalin was still nominally a member was the most powerful organ of government and made its decisions unchecked by the Communist Party. An observer at most of the sessions of the Bureau remarks that Stalin played a very colourless part in its discussions. "Stalin never took part in a discussion till it was ended. He was silent and listened attentively. Then when all had spoken, he would get up and say in a few words what was in effect the opinion of the majority and his view would be adopted. In this way he managed to make the members of the *Politbureau* think that it was his advice which had been taken." [1]

[1] Boris Bajanof: *Avec Staline dans le Kremlin.*

Stalin won over Kamenef and Zinovief to his side. He allowed them to think that they could use him in an intrigue against Trotsky. Trotsky by his overbearing manner had not made himself agreeable to the other two Jewish leaders. They might be smaller men but they were not dirt. They were as good revolutionaries as he was and they were convinced they were better Leninists. Ambition also (in others) was a fault. And Trotsky was dangerously ambitious. He did not share his counsels with other men. He brooded apart. When he spoke it was ebulliently and authoritatively, as if the comrades should at once run to do his bidding.

Stalin intended to play one Jew off against another. There is a quaint arithmetic which once went the rounds in the Near East: one Greek is equal to two Jews; one Armenian is equal to two Greeks. Stalin must have had Armenian blood in his veins. In cunning the Russian revolution did not turn up one Jew who was the equal of Stalin.

He dealt cynically with Kamenef, Zinovief and Trotsky, but at the same time he engaged in positive constructive intrigue for the making of his career in the revolution. As general secretary of the Party, he was in a position to pick out men for preferment and service. He proved to be a good judge of character. He knew exactly on what human elements in the Communist Party he could build. Thus in these early days he picked out V. M. Molotof, whom he made second secretary of the Party.

Molotof, who has risen to a position only second to Stalin, was unlike the screaming demagogues of the first revolution. He was a quiet, industrious, heavy vegetarian, an ideal conventional husband and

father, a man who did not drink, and spent sixteen
hours a day at his desk. His slow, clumsy gait
obtained for him the nick-name of "Stone-bottom."
Stalin seemed to give him a wink. "You and I,
Stone-bottom, will take over the apparatus of Party
management and make it work properly." Molotof,
well-educated, quiet and conventional, may not
altogether have liked the uncouthness of his master,
but he was signalled for a career and he was grateful.
In making the Party Stalin's he would also make it
his own. He was a capable bureaucrat who could
have served the Tsardom well in a high administrative post. He was assiduous. When Stone-bottom
took his seat, no one could push him off. Stalin owes
more to him than to any other of his assistants.

Trotsky, on the pedestal of his own greatness,
could not quite get the range of Molotof. Molotof
was a small man. He was rather pleased when Lenin
rebuked Molotof for some "impudent" remark
questioning Trotsky's loyalty to the Party. But he
did not grasp that Stalin, by the aid of this industrious
and hostile assistant, might some day make a majority
in the Party against him. It appeared to Trotsky at
the time that the chief personal force against him was
Zinovief. Kamenef ranged himself for a middle
course. He was jocular and cynical. One could not
say for certain which way he was going.

Stalin made rapid progress but his intrigue was
unexpectedly interrupted. Lenin who had been
buried before he died, so to speak, suddenly rose
and made a partial recovery. He came like a ghost
to trouble the ways of the living. All the leading
comrades greeted their Ilyitch with exaggerated
enthusiasm. All of them, even Trotsky, must have

been mightily disquieted. It was as if a dying King had struggled into the next room and found his sons trying on his crown. But little is known of the state of mind of the resurrected Lenin. He did not do very much. One imagines the comrades saying to him, like the Grand Inquisitor to the risen Christ, "You have written your Gospel. You must not add one word to it."

Someone has expressed it in exaggerated phrase: "He steered Russia with a paralysed arm." But he did not do much. He did not even remove Stalin, who was the prime cause of disaffection within the Party. He was unable to give any clear guidance as to who should be his successor. Apparently he still nursed the delusion that a revolution in the West of Europe would come about speedily and thus Marxism as Karl Marx contemplated it would be consummated.

But Trotsky and Lenin, though they had never been entirely of one mind, became nearer. Lenin's mind was cloudy and he did not see his way in Russia. He had inaugurated the distressing N.E.P. but did not have a plan for the future. Electrification had been stillborn and was almost a national joke. Trotsky's group were for the most part Jewish intellectuals, or revolutionaries who had spent their political exile in the West, or radicals with Western education and culture. They differed from most of the other Marxists in Russia in that they had read Karl Marx. But they viewed Russia with a certain contempt. It was a filthy, swinish country that could have no glorious future as a Socialist State. The peasants were antipathetic to them. A revolution had to be made in Russia. They never doubted that, but once the revolution was made their Russian task seemed to have been accomplished. It was futile to go on building up a new State, for when all Europe was in revolution there would be the much larger problem of organising one undivided Marxist State out of the whole continent. Russia would be administered not from Moscow but from Berlin or Geneva or some such suitable centre for all Europe.

At this time there seemed some immediate prospect of an extension of the revolution into Europe. Germany was in a problematic situation and the country was seething with Communism. Many of Trotsky's followers rushed off from Moscow to make revolution in Germany. Lenin in converse with Trotsky was afforded an excuse for not using the golden moments of his restoration to deal with the Russian question.

Yet even for Trotsky, though he did not admit it, the Russian question had become more urgent. If Trotsky was to regain control of the revolution the power of Stalin must be dispersed. Lenin must be made to remove Stalin from the secretariat of the Party. He set forth to achieve this in a roundabout manner, first of all acting upon the sympathies of Lenin's fussy wife. Mme. Lenin was persuaded that Stalin was preparing a *coup d'état* and she anxiously set to work to spy on the Georgian and report all his doings to her husband. One day when she got on to the telephone to Stalin he told her that she was a meddlesome bitch or something worse, something foul and brutal and quite unprintable.

The first energy of Lenin's recovery had spent itself. He was confined to his room and helplessly neurasthenical. He did not know how to deal with the gossip that was brought to him. It is said that Lenin wrote a letter to Stalin reproaching him with his rudeness but no copy of the letter exists. At the same time the Trotsky group managed to suggest to Lenin that Stalin was acting as if he, Lenin, had ceased to count in Russia. He had taken matters into his own hands in the repression of the Georgian movement for revolutionary independence.

What would Lenin do? The leaders in Moscow dwelt among rumours. Rumour said that Lenin was preparing to come to the Party and move the expulsion of Stalin. Mme. Lenin was sure that he was about to act. Kamenef wavered for a moment to the side of Trotsky. The counter intrigue was helped by the fact that Stalin had got a chill on the stomach and had been obliged to go to the country to rest and recover. This was not a political illness.

Trotsky charged Kamenef to go to Tiflis and proceed in the local party against Stalin. Trotsky sent Lenin a mass of materials concerning Stalin's highhandedness in the Caucasus, in case he intended to denounce Stalin to the Party. Lenin's secretary brought the papers back as his master was incapable of any such decided action. But the sick Lenin had evidently a desperate last-hour consciousness of the fact that he had made a mistake in giving Stalin power: According to Mme. Lenin her husband had dictated a letter to Stalin breaking off all further relationship. Stalin wrote a letter of apology to Lenin. The Georgian's position was in grave danger. Whether he was at all frightened is doubtful. Probably he would have wriggled out of the diffi-

culty because Trotsky weakly declared that he would
not himself oppose Stalin in the Party.

In any case a *Deus ex machina* intervened to save
Stalin from wrath. On his way to Tiflis, Kamenef
received a telegram: "Lenin is paralysed. Neither
speaks nor writes." So when he arrived at Tiflis he
did the exact opposite of what Trotsky had instructed.
He confirmed the measures of Stalin in Georgia in
the name of the Communist Party.

Now Lenin was a living corpse. He babbled
incoherently, with saliva trickling down his chin. A
hell was provided for him. He could read and
understand and hear but he could not say or
act. His wife's grief was rudely disturbed by the
return to Moscow of the enraged Stalin. He made
her eat her words, return the letter of apology he
had sent and destroy the letter addressed to him
which was waiting for Lenin's signature. He threatened to denounce her before the whole of the
Party and, unlike a woman, it must be said, she
gave in.

From this time on, the war of Stalin upon Trotsky
was not waged under cover. It did not cease till
Trotsky was banished from Russia. Stalin had
gathered the power of the Communist Party into
his hands and he proceeded to use it. A majority
was mobilised against Trotsky in the Party. The
Triumvirate emerged. Stalin, Kamenef and Zinovief
seized the executive power. Trotsky unable to
proceed with his personal programme, began his
long career of *malade imaginaire*. He ran a temperature for which the doctors could not ascribe a
cause. At the close of 1923 he decided to go to
Sukhum, in the Caucasus for his health, a resort

decidedly remote from Stalin and the seat of government. It was in effect voluntary exile. It is not
probable that his high temperature would have
prevented his remaining in Moscow had his position
there been tolerable.

CHAPTER XII

LENIN'S lips were watched for a long time but he did not speak. According to Ossendowsky he made a final effort at the moment of death and mumbled the words "Christ" and "Love" but there seems no warrant for that and it is unlikely enough. He was never troubled by religious doubts; he was not an agnostic. His atheism was clear-cut and positive. Disease is a human tragedy which has to be met, and he met it with what fortitude he could summon, bereft of religion. The materialist on his deathbed should have uttered a last word of guidance for Materialism.

Actually he left behind what has been called his last testament. It was not a bequest of his worldly goods but some attempt to dispose of his political power. This document is not in existence because by consent of the leaders of the Communist Party it was destroyed and considered not to have been written. The Comrades gave him a great State funeral; they embalmed his body; they built for him a monumental dwelling place and shrine. As it were they canonised him as the first saint of Atheism and made his tomb a place of pilgrimage, but they destroyed his testament.

There was good human reason for that. In his testament he made no choice of a successor but instead offended each of the leaders in turn. The reading of this will of the revered Ilyitch provided an interesting moment in the deliberations of the Party. The death of Lenin hid the discord within

the Party in a cloud of sentimentalism. Nominally
it had caused unity, actually it had done nothing of
the kind. Stalin telegraphed the news of the death
to Trotsky but he did not want Trotsky rushing
back with all the army behind him, and advised him
to remain and continue his treatment. Trotsky at
that moment still had the power to make a military
coup. But the danger to Stalin was less than in all
probability he imagined. Trotsky was not gifted
with the power to seize great opportunities. Instead
of returning forthwith to Moscow he lingered among
the palms of Sukhum fidgeting irresolutely.

A delegation from the Central Committee composed
of Frunze, Tomsky and others then arrived at
Sukhum inviting him to co-operate in making certain
changes in the war department. "This was sheer
farce," says Trotsky. "The changes of personnel
in the war department had been going on at full
speed behind my back for some time." Stalin was
busily getting rid of Trotsky's friends and replacing
them by the "heroes of Tsaritsin." The Jewish
leader was letting things slide.

Frunze, who had been sent to him, was a Jew
from Pishpek, in Central Asia. Pishpek is now
renamed Frunze after him. Stalin again used one
Jew against another. A nod is as good as a wink.
Frunze saw himself as designate commissary for
war in Trotsky's place. When Trotsky did at last
come to Moscow he found that he still had sufficient
military backing for a *coup d'état.* It was Frunze
who made it dangerous for him.

Trotsky preferred to wait for the reading of
Lenin's last will and testament. If, as he believed,
Lenin had nominated him as the inheritor of his

power, he might win Russia politically, by acclamation, without recourse to violence.

The testament was actually in the hands of Stalin and Kamenef, and it is probable that they knew what was in it before they read it. Bazhanof, who had been appointed assistant secretary under Molotof, describes Stalin's face as he saw it during the reading of the will. "Crouching on one of the presidential benches, he looked shrunken and pathetic. I watched him attentively. In spite of his self-control and feigned calm one could see clearly that he felt his destiny was at stake. The words— *to be or not to be*, were written in the lines of his tense figure."

Lenin's words regarding Stalin were read to the Central Committee of the Party by Kamenef who was making the recital of the document. We have already quoted them. Lenin said that Stalin was too rough in his ways, and he intended to propose to the comrades that they should relieve him of his post as secretary of the Party. There was a clear intention on the part of Lenin to warn the comrades against Stalin, but the denunciation did not go far enough to be effective. Neither his orthodoxy as a party man nor his loyalty to Lenin were called to question.

Both Kamenef and Zinovief were treated somewhat negligibly by Lenin, as if, in fact, they were not presidential timber and need not be considered seriously. He referred to their wavering during the October, 1917, revolution and that was damning.

Concerning Trotsky, Lenin was far from clear. It is probable that the testament was written not at the time of his greatest exasperation with Stalin.

Possibly it was not all written at one sitting. Just
before his second seizure he was near enough to
Trotsky to have come to a clear decision about
him.

"Comrades Trotsky and Stalin are the two most
able men in the present Central Committee," read
Kamenef. "Their rivalry might quite innocently
lead to a split.[1] Comrade Trotsky is perhaps the
most talented of the leaders but he is too conceited.
And then he is not a Bolshevik."[2]

This last statement proved fatal to Trotsky's
chances. Stalin got a punch on the nose, nothing
more, but Trotsky got his in the solar plexus.

Trotsky rather slurs over the impression that
Lenin did not altogether trust him. In his autobiography he recounts how on one occasion, in July,
1919, Lenin gave him a blank cheque, a form of
order signed by himself with a blank space in which
Trotsky could write in anything he wished. "You
can have as many of these as you like," said Lenin.
And he certainly would never have given Stalin a
blank order of that kind. It would have been too
dangerous. It may have been done to flatter Trotsky
whose vanity was in constant need of food. Trotsky
would do little with it, but it would make him feel
that he was the man "whom the King delighted to
honour." According to Maxim Gorky, Lenin thought
highly of Trotsky's organising abilities. "And yet,"
said he, "he isn't one of us. With is but not of us.
He is ambitious. There is something of Lassalle in
him, something which isn't good."[3]

[1] Taken from the Report of the American Trade Delegation,
1928.
[2] Taken from *Stalin* by S. Dmitrievsky.
[3] Maxim Gorky: *V. T. Lenin.*

It was Trotsky's cue to get up and make a strong speech, taking leadership into his hands on the strength of personality and following. But Zinovief arranged it that the only person discussed was Stalin. Stalin stood up and addressed the comrades:—"I know I am sharp and rough. But what are you going to do about that? I was born that way." And he was applauded.

Zinovief made a rhetorical appeal to the committee. "No one doubts that every slightest word of Lenin's has for us the force of law," said he. "But there is one matter in which we are happy to admit that his apprehensions are not confirmed. I speak of the question of the general secretary of the Party."

Kamenef backed Zinovief. Trotsky said nothing, contenting himself by showing his immense disdain by making faces and gestures. The discussion as to whether, taking Lenin's advice, Stalin should be replaced was shelved, a closure being voted informally by show of hands.

The will afforded little political or moral advantage to Trotsky. It was his moment to strike at Stalin but either he was paralysed by Lenin's words or he simply lacked the pluck. The will was waste paper as far as he was concerned, and he did not object to the proposal that its existence should be hidden from the Party as a whole and from the Russian people. When its contents were divulged on hearsay by the emigré Press in Paris and Berlin Trotsky authoritatively denied that there had been such a document. In his autobiography Trotsky now gives his version of the will. The essence of it according to Trotsky was that Stalin be removed in order to avoid a split in the Party. If so, why did he not press for it?

The crafty Stalin was not content with the way the question of removing him from office had been shelved. He employed a clever bluff. The Thirteenth Congress of the Party took place in June and shortly afterwards at a plenary session of the Central Committee, Stalin begged to be relieved of his duties. And Trotsky, Kamenef and Zinovief and all the delegates of the local parties asked him to remain. Thus he remained by the will of the Party. Next year Stalin repeated this gesture, knowing full well that he would not be taken at his word.

Trotsky, asked by a friend to define Stalin, replied: "Stalin is the outstanding mediocrity in the Party."[1]

One must understand Trotsky in the sense that a clever card player may yet be a mediocrity.

Trotsky also quotes an opinion of Bukharin regarding Stalin. "Stalin's first quality is laziness; his second is an implacable jealousy."

Trotsky says he was suited to play second or third fiddle. He points out that Stalin is uncultured, knows no foreign languages. Of himself Trotsky has the highest opinion. He felt himself equal with Lenin in the revolution. "I had my own views, my own methods of carrying out a decision once it had been adopted. Lenin knew this well enough and respected it. That was why he understood only too well that I was not suited for executing commissions. When he needed men to carry out his instructions, he turned to someone else." He turned to this "lazy" Stalin. It may be remarked that those who are willing to serve often go further than those who cannot.

[1] Leon Trotsky: *My Life.*

Trotsky's disdain for the lesser lights of the revolution, his proud isolation, his contemptuous passivity, helped him not a whit. He had an enemy and a rival in Stalin. Trotsky's hands no less that Stalin's were red with the blood of Russia. They were both in the midst of social war. And now they were at war with one another. It was a fact to be faced.

Stalin, confirmed as general secretary of the Party, continued energetically his task of converting the apparatus into his own personal instrument. In due course he would dispose of Zinovief and Kamenef as he had of Trotsky. But he had not finished with Trotsky. Trotsky had a great number of enthusiastic admirers. Some of these were more ready for a fray than Trotsky was. They were organising and conspiring. It appeared that even against his will Trotsky might be made to mount his white horse again and prance in triumph over a confounded opposition. There were some critical days.

"For two weeks we all expected a *coup*," says Bessedovsky. "Trotsky might, like Pilsudsky, seize the reins of power. It was literally a question of minutes. The letter of Ovseyenko to the *Politbureau* that ' if a hand is laid on Trotsky, the whole Red Army will rise to protect him ' made the Stalin faction very nervous. The catastrophe might come any minute. But Trotsky was faint-hearted. Stalin called Frunze from Kharkhof. In a short while the danger was passed and Trotsky was hopelessly compromised.

Even then the Trotsky legend endured. In the revolution, the name most coupled with that of the dead Lenin was his. Still the names Lenin and

Trotsky meant the revolution. Doubt must be cast
on the reliability and orthodoxy of Trotsky and at
the same time the greatness and unique character
of Lenin must be magnified. In Leningrad, in
Moscow, and in the provinces, scores of preliminary
secret conferences had been held to discuss Trotsky's
position. "When the secret preparations were over,"
says Trotsky, "at a signal from *Pravda* a campaign
against Trotskyism burst forth simultaneously on
all platforms, in all pages and columns. It was a
majestic spectacle of a kind. . . . It was a great
shock to the large mass of the Party. I lay in bed
with a temperature and remained silent."

This was in the autumn of 1924. Even if the rôle
of Trotsky had been adequately defended, which
it was not, his position in the revolution had been
cast in doubt. The legend had been to some extent
dispelled. At the same time there was a conspiracy
to exaggerate the greatness of Lenin. The dead
body had been lying in state; that same body,
embalmed, should lie in state forever. A great tomb,
like the counter-balance to the Sepulchre of Christ,
should be built for him in the Red Square. Trostky
protested. In a socialistic revolution no man could
be as great as they were making out Lenin to be.
"They used the corpse of Lenin against me," says
Trotsky. Exactly. Stalin was arranging that no name
such as Trotsky could be coupled with that of Lenin
in the annals of the revolution.

Stalin did more. He made Lenin s books into a
Bible of the revolution, a sacred Gospel. In this he
went against the spirit of Leninism. For Lenin had
been for the democratisation of the revolution. In
his opinion, two men's counsels had been better

than one. He had always been loth to proscribe any of the comrades. He felt that the Party had to live by its collective wisdom rather than through the guidance of one man. But Stalin, for his own ends converted Bolshevism into a theocracy. His training for priesthood in his adolescence may have helped him when, as it were, he invented Commandments of Lenin. "I am the Lord thy God, thou shalt have no other gods but me." There was no room for Trotskyists. One must be either a Leninist or an enemy of the Soviet.

In the following January Trotsky was relieved of his duties as People's Commissary for War.

CHAPTER XIII

THE triumvirate supported by Dzherzhinsky, Bukharin, Ordzhonikidze, Molotof, Bubnof and others now held supreme control. A successor was found to Lenin in comrade Rikof, a man who had promised to become a capable administrator. But he was best known for his love of the bottle. The slang word for vodka became *rikovka*. The Trotsky faction within the Party met secretly to organise resistance, closely watched by spies from the other side. Now that the victory over Trotsky seemed to have been won, Zinovief and Kamenef began to consider how they could get rid of Stalin. They were not followers of Stalin and they believed that if it came to a count they would be found to have the bulk of the votes in the Party. If upon occasion they could avail themselves of the Trotsky vote they might win.

Stalin believed that he had made it impossible for these two to return to the Trotsky fold. He had allowed them to do most of the denouncing of Trotsky. "The man who says that Trotskyism could have any legitimate place in the Bolshevik party is himself not a Bolshevik," declared Zinovief in 1925. "Trotsky has become the symbol of all that is directed against the Party," wrote Kamenef about the same time. "We must employ all means to stop the infection of this anti-bolshevism."

These words, carefully preserved in the archives, were used with deadly effect by Stalin when the two sharers of his power did eventually go over to Trotsky and attempt to make alliance against him.

Actually, Kamenef and Zinovief were losing their supporters rapidly. Stalin had dawned upon the younger comrades as their leader. The anti-semitic strain is ineradicable even in Red Russians. Neither of the Jewish leaders had a personality that widely recommended itself. For one thing, like Trotsky they enjoyed the luxury which the revolution had brought them. Stalin, remaining a *sans culotte*, had avoided the reproach of having benefited personally by the change of circumstances. He wore no collar; he looked a proletarian, even at the seat of power. Then by encouraging the young and the outsiders he had appealed to the nationalism latent in the Russians. And he used the G.P.U., the old Cheka renamed, to get rid of many who were thwarting him.

He outwitted Kamenef and Zinovief in many ways. Thus when they brought him their own nominee to be head of the Moscow party, Uglianof, he gave his consent with seeming great reluctance. They thought Uglianof was their man, but actually he was Stalin's.

Trotsky was kept without a post until May when he was tested to see whether he would be content with a much smaller part in the government. The army had been taken from him, how would he like to administer the department of Foreign Concessions? It was found that he had become much humbler. He accepted the chairmanship of the Concessions Board with readiness, and actually he obtained work which suited his abilities more than the control of the fighting forces. Trotsky had an international mind. In no sense was he a Russian, a man without a country from the first. What he brought to the revolution and what Lenin probably most prized in him was his broad international vision. His new post brought him into practical contact with the realities of the West. He gathered about him his new international clientele the chief of whom were Krassin and Rakovsky.

Kamenef and Zinovief were also ardent internationalists, but Stalin, at that time at least, was not. His policy was reconstructive, domestic and agrarian. Kamenef and Zinovief made internationalist speeches against the background of the opposition. But that opposition was of similar fabric to their own and they seemed to fade into it and become part of it. Stalin, having canvassed the Party and the *Politbureau*, found that he could mobilise a majority against them and very soon after they began to contest his personal political programme, he showed his power. In the autumn of 1925 they were outvoted and removed from office.

Stalin held the Fourteenth Congress in the hollow of his hand and had the power even then to have excluded Trotsky from the Party. He told the comrades how at an earlier period Kamenef and Zinovief had pressed him to have Trotsky excluded. "But we could not agree with comrades Kamenef and Zinovief, because we knew that the policy of the removal of members had great risk for the Party. The method of removal—the method of letting blood, and they demanded blood—is dangerous and infectious. To-day we remove one, to-morrow another, the next day a third, and what would be left of the Party?"

Actually what Stalin meant was that it was not safe to begin removing members at that time. He was very cautious in his dealings with his rivals for power. In this he belied the judgment of Lenin, who was of opinion that Stalin was too impetuous and apt to fire his gun before it was loaded. He did seize an early opportunity to finish with Trotsky completely, did not remove him from the Party, did not even have him assassinated, which would not have been difficult for him to compass, simply contented himself by removing him from the administration.

Zinovief and Kamenef were playing their hands badly in their bid for power. One can see they were defective in judgment. They had a sneaking belief that Trotsky was a greater man than Stalin. Possibly the showiness of Trotsky, who was eternally posing, deceived them. Stalin still looked like a small man and an upstart. They took him at his face value and could not believe that he held the future in his hands.

In Trotsky, however, they did not at that time find much support. His temperature went up again and he sought a warmer and safer climate. Zinovief and Kamenef crawled back to Stalin and made repentance. Stalin forgave them but did not at once admit them back to office. They had to be content with profitable sinecures for the time being.

Trotsky's position remained very painful for him. He could not recover an inch of his lost ground. Yet he could not brook frustration. It reacted terribly on his nerves. His constant state of agitation no doubt did play havoc with his health. His illness was evidently psychological. In failure he did not say to his friends "I am losing the battle," but "I feel so ill." He used ill-health somewhat as Kerensky had used it. In the new year, 1926, he began to think of going to Germany "to consult a specialist." He applied for permission. The G.P.U. would not sanction the trip but Trotsky found he still had enough power to over-ride their objection. He went to Berlin, talked about his temperature to the doctors, they removed his tonsils, but still the temperature endured. That high temperature remains though without visible cause or credible diagnosis. Germany, however, proved a tonic for the Red leader. He returned to Russia in a vigorous mood and interposed emphatically in affairs of State.

The behaviour of the British T.U.C. at the close of the General Strike of May, 1926, had convinced Trotsky that the Russian communists must break with the Trade Union leaders of Great Britain. Zinovief, after wavering for a while, once more came to Trotsky's side. A vigorous agitation against Stalin ensued, with the Georgian using every means at his disposal to suffocate free speech. Trotsky's adherents met secretly to make a programme of their own and start a party within the Party. By advocating an increase of wages for the working masses and an abolition of the taxes on poor peasants they hoped to win a hold on the country. The members of the second party used every occasion in the official assemblies to make factional speeches. These speeches were sometimes printed and discussed in public, an infringement of the rule of the Communist Party. But Stalin was not passive in dealing with this conspiracy.

"There cannot be two parties; there can only be one Party—just as there is not room for both Trotskyists and Leninists. There is only the party of Lenin in Russia." He mobilised the party to crush the opposition, and in October, 1926, took place the general engagement between the conflicting forces. In the face of an overwhelming majority and the threat that they would be totally excluded from the Party, the opposition surrendered. "The opposition was obliged to beat a retreat," says Trotsky, and he called it an armistice.

Trotsky this time remained on the scene waiting for another opening. It came with Stalin's intervention in the progress of the Chinese revolution. According to Trotsky, Stalin misunderstood the Chinese situation, made alliance with the wrong Chinese leader in the person of Chiang Kai-shek and thus betrayed the Chinese proletariat. Excitement ran high and the opposition dared to raise its head again. Still the leader of this opposition did not know how to profit by the excitement. Probably the Russian masses were almost indifferent to the lot of the Chinese communists.

Kamenef and Zinovief again flirted with the opposition. The movement gained ground again. Such grievances abounded in Russia as are not to be found in any other land. The dragooning of the workers, the bullying of the peasants had bred a discontent which might flare if Trotsky applied the match. It seemed to the man on the street that he could not fare worse under Trotsky than under Stalin. Street demonstrations in favour of Trotsky and Zinovief became frequent. The first of them, in Leningrad, gave a new name to the movement.

Zinovief accepted the plaudits of the factory workers
and the rabble of the old capital and the official
Press pinned on him and his friends the name
"Leningradtsi."

Zinovief, for a moment, was intoxicated by his
success, but Trotsky poured cold water on his
enthusiasm. As ever he feared to come out into
the open and fight. The demonstration "would
not prevent the apparatus making short work
of us. On this score I had no illusions . . . it
was bound to suggest to the ruling faction the
necessity of speeding up the destruction of the
opposition."

The Leningrad demonstration took place in
October, 1927. It was repeated shortly afterwards
in Moscow on the occasion of the tenth anniversary
of the Bolshevik revolution. There was rough
handling of the crowds. Trotsky's automobile was
shot at. Someone with an axe jumped on the step
of the car and shattered the windscreen. It seemed
to Trotsky that a bloody end was being prepared for
himself and his sympathisers. It is possible he was
right in his judgment at this point. Had he decided
to lead a militant party of revolt he would have been
beaten just the same. He had left it too late. He was
frightened by the extent of his turbulent success.
In November he asked that no more large meetings
should be organised. Stalin answered by expelling
Trotsky from the Party. Zinovief hurriedly surrendered. In December, at the fifteenth Congress
of the Party, Stalin obtained the exclusion of the
whole of the Trotsky faction *en bloc*, and the expelled
were placed at the disposal of the G.P.U. as enemies
of the revolution.

Trotsky was now treated as a counter-revolutionary, and but for his numerous following would undoubtedly have been shot. Instead he was banished to a remote part of Russian Central Asia. The agents of the G.P.U. came to his house, and he thought he could resist them passively. He refused to dress or budge. They had to put his boots on his feet and forcibly clothe him. He had expected a demonstration in his favour and perhaps a rescue on the way to the station, but the police had tricked both him and the crowds as to the time of his departure. He was deported 3,000 miles from Moscow with ease and celerity.

That was in January, 1928. Trotsky kept up a large correspondence with his friends and adherents all the year. He still remained the head of the opposition faction in Russia, gave it advice and encouraged its development. Stalin's answer to that was to withhold all further mail addressed to him. In December an agent of the G.P.U. visited him bearing an ultimatum: either he must stop directing the opposition or measures would be taken to isolate him from political life. It must have seemed to Trotsky that this was an empty threat. At 3,000 miles from the seat of government, deprived of his correspondence, he was effectively isolated. Trotsky refused to give a reply on the ground that the message was verbal. Let the G.P.U. send a written ultimatum and he would give a written reply. He did, however, address a statement of his position to the Central Committee. He evidently thought that the alternative to his banishment was prison.

The agent of the G.P.U. did not take the letter. It was despatched by courier. The agent waited in

attendance upon Trotsky. A month later he re-
appeared at Trotsky's house with armed guards. An
order had come for his deportation out of the
territories of the U.S.S.R. No one tried to save him.
On February 12th, 1929, the recalcitrant Red leader
was set down in Constantinople. Stalin was rid of
him for a long spell.

CHAPTER XIV

THE stumbling block of the revolution, up to Stalin's dictatorship, has been the problem of the peasantry. In a sense, Lenin overlooked the peasantry. He did not include the peasantry in the proletariat. If he had done so, a dictatorship of the proletariat in Russia must have meant a dictatorship by the peasantry since they outnumber the rest of the workers by ten to one. In Lenin's view the peasantry must be made to support the proletariat but not control it. The peasantry must be made into good Communists and must be divorced from their traditional piety. And to that end in Lenin's time an intensive propaganda was carried on in the vast rural areas.

Envy was encouraged. The poor peasants were set against the rich peasants and the landless against those who had property. Village churches were pulled down or converted into clubs or cinemas. Training for the priesthood was stopped so that there should be no young priests to take the place of the old ones when they died. Education of the children was taken out of the hands of the priests and given to Communistic teachers who were sent up country for the purpose.

This cannot be said to have been very successful. Militant Communism, the raids, the plundering of the farms alienated the peasantry, rich and poor alike. When that was stopped and the N.E.P. was introduced the peasants began to sell their crops again but the rich multiplied. Taxes, were however, not taken in the new currency, but in kind, and that again alienated the peasantry and spurred them to crafty combination. The answer to taxes in kind was an unorganised boycot. The peasants sowed just enough for their personal needs and to feed the stock. The towns, that is the proletariat, languished on short rations.

The Soviet answer to the boycot was a forcible confiscation of whatever grain the commissaries could lay hands on. It went too far. The peasants fed themselves as best they could but they had not enough over to feed their stock. So they sold their stock to the butcher or killed it and ate it themselves. First there was a glut of meat and then an appalling shortage of both meat and grain. The rab-kors, that is Communist propagandists and teachers, were murdered in any number. The whole peasantry except some of the poorest and the debauched were hostile to Moscow. The hostility was not dangerous, because the peasants could not combine and fight. There never was any danger of a Peasants' War. After all the scythe cannot be matched against the machine gun. But the economic position was precarious. The area of land sown had become 30 per cent less than the pre-war area and crops had depreciated to an even greater extent.

Stalin and his colleagues were opportunists with regard to the country. Where bread was concerned they had no very fixed principles unless the fact that they must have bread can be considered a principle. Stalin had learned from Lenin: if one method will not work abandon it and try another. In 1924–5 he tried a new policy. He leaned upon what came to be known as the opposition of the Right. The Rights, Bukharin, Rikof, Tomsky, believed in a policy of maximum concessions to the peasant proprietor. Bukharin advised the peasants to get rich, which is a complete contradiction of Communism. "Peasants! Get rich!" said he. The persecution of the rich peasants was withdrawn and the poorer peasants who had been so much encouraged to attack their masters were no longer favoured.

At the fourteenth Party Congress in 1905 the peasant proprietors were given the right to lease additional land and to hire additional labour for their fields. Stalin even went so far as to offer a delegation of peasant farmers a form of leasehold title to their lands for periods of forty years and more, but under pressure from the Left, that is the Trotsky faction, he was obliged to retract this astonishing capitulation of principle.[1]

But the policy of supporting the richer and more responsible peasants was not abandoned for some years. Agriculture picked up; the stock increased again; the sown area increased by 33 per cent. There was meat and bread again in Moscow.

Then the preliminaries for the Five Year Plan were set in motion. At first only the industrialisation of Russia was planned. In order to restart industries and equip new ones it became necessary to raise an internal loan The Party used all the political machinery at its disposal to raise this loan. Its operations remind one of British finance in the reign of Charles I, the time of benevolences and forced contributions. The proletariat was mulcted in their wages; the petty trader under the eye of the G.P.U. was practically forced to take up bonds. Everyone who makes the least extra money is under the

[1] S. Dmitrievsky: *Stalin.*

surveillance of the G.P.U. and in danger of being arrested for speculation. There was the curious paradox of a Communist country seeking capital.

In the towns the policy of forced contributions was successful. But when it was applied to the country there was widespread resistance, some hundred thousand village Hampdens withstanding the petty tyrants of their fields. A few years of non-interference with ordinary normal farming had put money in the hands of the peasantry again, perhaps not very much but enough to be accounted wealth in impoverished Russia. The village Hampdens of Russia refused to give money to the government they detested. All the work of the Right faction of the Party was undone. Stalin sent his underlings to collect contributions by force from the richer peasants and they reverted to boycott. They cut the acreage under cultivation and sold their stock, bringing about in a very short time a food crisis in all the towns. The peasants buried their grain and their potatoes and lived on their secret food hoards while the towns starved. This was met by raiding expeditions, arrests, shootings and something not unlike a civil war when one side is unarmed.

Once more the Communist Party was at war with its food. It came to a deadlock. The proletariat may be pretty low but it will not eat dead peasant. The Right faction of the Party was opposed to this terrorisation of the village, but it was hardly possible to go back to the richer peasants, the kulaks as they call them opprobriously, and says: "All right, carry on!"

The programme of industrialisation also demanded a settlement of the food question. You cannot run

large scale manufacture with the half-starved workers
spending the whole of their spare time standing in
lines waiting for rations.

With the banishment of Trotsky in January, 1927,
Stalin ceased to require the support of the Rights.
In a quiet and methodical way he began to underpin
the leaders. They had very considerable following
in Russia, which was tired of Communist extremism
and turned with relief to state capitalism and any
possible compromise between the old time regime
and socialism. He branded their policy as "petty
bourgeois liberalism." Their strength, as he saw it,
consisted in the strength of the petty bourgeois
elements in the country, the pressure on the Party
by these elements and by the richer peasants. "The
victory of the Right would have meant the complete
disarming of the proletariat, the arming of the
capitalist element in the villages and possibly a
restoration of capitalism in the U.S.S.R."

The G.P.U. was set to watch the sympathisers
with this programme and when almost the whole of
their support in the country and in the Party had been
cut away from under their feet Stalin got rid of the
leaders. It was cleverly done. Tomsky and Rikof,
unaware of what had happened to their support, just
fell to the ground. Poor drunken Rikof, in Lenin's
shoes, president of the *Sovnarkom* and proud of it.
wept piteously over his discomfiture. But he had to
go. Stalin had decided to disembarrass himself even
of Rikof's nominal authority as the head of the
Soviets and therefore of republican Russia.

Thus with Trotsky and the faction of the Left
disposed of on the one hand, and Rikof and Tomsky
and the faction of the Right disposed of on the other,

Stalin occupied a central position founded more on his personal ascendancy than on settled policy. He became "dictator of Russia," though it is fair to say that that is an appellation given him not by himself but by the journalists of the West. He was very careful to preserve the appearances of being still a comrade on the level with the humblest citizen of the republic. Thus he did not occupy a presidential chair either at the meetings of the *Sovnarkom* nor of the Party. At the *Politbureau*, the chair of Lenin was left vacant. The members ranged themselves about the long red table with its crimson cloth. Stalin did not preside. He allowed Molotof to do that while he himself sat on his left. Afterward when Molotof was made chairman of the Economic Council, Rudzutak, commissary for communications, presided. Stalin took his position merely as a member of the bureau though all the rest knew that the whole executive power was in his hands.

Still the peasant problem was not solved. It got to the point when it was logical to say that the Communist Party must either solve the peasant problem or face a complete economic failure. Stalin searched the works of Lenin for guidance, or was it for confirmation of his own intentions? In Lenin, he found the following:

"All the means of large-scale production are in the hands of the State, and the powers of the State are in the hands of the proletariat; there is the alliance of this same proletariat with the many millions of the middle-class and poorer peasants; there is the assured leadership of these peasants by the proletariat . . ."[1]

[1] Lenin's Works, vol. xviii

From that Stalin deduced "the labouring masses of the peasantry as a reserve force for the proletariat." He went further. He wrote his conclusion in these words: "The proletariat, having secured power, can make use of this reserve force in order to link up industry with agriculture."

In short Stalin decided to proletarianise the peasantry. The desperate situation in the villages helped him. The horses were dead; the logical substitute was the tractor. The horse, it will be readily understood, is a bad communist. The tractor is a much better instrument of Marxism. The tractor changes the village community into a gang and the peasant labourer into a proletarian. The peasant becomes, in a sense, a factory operative, with the field and the machine as his factory.

A new agricultural programme was developed on the basis of the tractor. Russia is as admirably suited for the use of agricultural machinery as Canada; perhaps more so. Its enormous area of grain producing land is as flat as a table. Russia is suited to large-scale farming and the mass production of wheat.

The chief difficulty, if it could be overcome, solved both an economic and a political problem. That difficulty was the petty ownership of land. Nominally, the peasants were, for the most part, in possession of the land. They believed they were the owners of it. The peasants, in addition to their many religious and pagan superstitions, have also an economic one: it is that God made the land for the peasant. Their avidity for ownership in land is inborn. When the first revolution took place it interested them chiefly as an opportunity to snatch

all the land they could from the sequestered land-
owners. When the Whites marched North, all they
asked for their support was legal title to the new
lands. The Reds when they won the civil war could
not expropriate the peasants though private ownership
of land was a contravention of their dogma. They
were forced to accept the *status quo* and wait their
opportunity for the socialisation of property in
agricultural land. Actually, they seemed to possess
their land; in political theory they were merely
a many million-fold tribe of squatters.

But the tractor is not suited to the ploughing of
small parcels of land. The Canadian unit, the section,
is a square mile. It is economical to drive a tractor,
furrow ten miles at a stretch and not turn round;
better still to drive twenty tractors in parallel furrows
for twenty miles. The larger the scale of employ,
the more economical the enterprise.

The use of the tractor might be limited to State
lands or the peasants might be organised in collectives
to use it. The decision was to make it all-Russian.
This decision was probably the greatest economic
step taken in the development of the Russian
revolution. Since the emancipation of the serfs
the lot of the peasant has not undergone a greater
change.

The formation of collectives using agricultural
became the dominant factor of the Five Year Plan.
At first it was scoffed at. Russia had no tractors and
no machinery for making tractors. Also she seemed
to have little money for buying agricultural machinery
on a large scale; nor did she have men who understood machinery nor repair shops. But then she did
have Stalin behind the plan, the will and the per-

sistence of the man who had subdued the revolution to his control.

The great plan did not end as so many Russian proposals are apt to do, in mere talk. It was not one of the paper schemes. Tractors were bought in large numbers in America and in England. Foreign engineers and skilled artisans were imported into the country. Plant for the manufacture of tractors was imported. Factories for making tractors were equipped. In two years from the outset the agricultural side of the Five Year Plan startled the depths of the sleeping Russian peasantry. A nation wide campaign against the peasant proprietor had got going. The peasants with land were being "beaten, bobbed and thumped" into surrendering their land to the collectives. Every means of intimidation and boycott were employed to force the landed peasants to come in. There were disturbances and impotent revolt, but these were put down with ruthlessness.

The poorer peasants saw emancipation in the collective; the richer ones saw the merging of their small fortune and position. Now something had been found which put reality into the class war of the peasants. The poor peasants hailed the tractor with song and dance, declaring that the toil of the ages had been overcome. The rich regarded it with morose faces. But there was nothing for it; the rich had to surrender.

So, peasant life as we know it was broken up. The new community became the collective. Village life was largely changed into camp life. The labourers on the soil became akin to workmen. The area under cultivation and the harvest taken increased at a

surprising pace. The government became richer and
obtained the means of buying still more machinery
and extending the development of the industrial side
of their programme.

The only doubts which may be cast on the success
of the collectives may be indicated in the following
questions:

(1) Did it pay to take away religion from the
peasant?

(2) Will it pay to debauch village life in changing
it to camp life?

(3) Will not the vast surplus peasant population
rendered idle by machinery displacing hand labour
become a menace in some other direction?

(4) Will the peasant serfs of the collectives who at
first enjoyed the novelty of the experiment, remain
permanently contented there?

Which questions bring me to the surmise that
Stalin is succeeding and is going somewhere, but he
does not yet know where. The purpose of the grain
surplus over and above the government's needs is
to ruin the grain markets of the West. But economic
war is not fair trading and is legitimately met by
the embargo. What then?

In the opening stages of success, despite the good
harvests, the population of Russia is kept on sparse
rations. The food they raise does not profit them
directly. There is the anomaly of the co-existence
of bumper harvests and bread lines. The propagandists ask the population to be patient. When the
Five Year Plan has all the foreign machinery it
requires, imports will decrease and it will be possible

to allow more own bread to remain in Russia. There is certainly a possibility overlooked by the propagandists and that is that as a result of a foreign embargo on the export of Russian wheat, prosperity and plenty might roll back beneficently upon the long-suffering Russian people.

CHAPTER XV

WHEN Stalin had got rid of Trotsky and reduced Kamenef and Zinovief to the position of humble if well-paid servants of the State, when he had disposed of Tomsky and the opposition of the Right, and removed the drunken figure of Rikof he became absolute and might well have come out on parade like a Napoleon or a Mussolini. But that was not his style. He took his triumph quietly, with circumspection. Still he remained General Secretary. *Gensek*, to use the Bolshevik jargon. Someone has remarked that the greatest parade may be an absence of parade. If so he has it. His pose is still the "comrade." No grandeur; no change of clothes. Does he wear his hair a trifle longer? Perhaps. But he does not brush it much. He is not a customer for the Red barber. At times, however, his abundant cloak, hanging free, gives him a certain majesty of appearance, as of an archpriest.

But he has now his country seat or summer residence. He lives in the house where Lenin died, outside Moscow, Gorki, a fine white house with Greek columns. It is a nice place with white walled rooms, pictures in gilded frames, armchairs and sofas upholstered in white and gold, antique marble vases, crimson curtains, palms and ferns in big pots. There are portraits of gentry of a bygone age. Not much has been disturbed since the original owners quitted the scene. Stalin lives there as if he had leased a furnished house for the season. He does not order the bourgeois luxury to be removed. Neither does he profit by it very much. It does not interest him. He sits in his own cabinet with masses of papers and books and works. Here for a while he tried to learn English, but gave it up, finding it too difficult. Sometimes he gets up and goes to another room and plays the pianola, which, it is said, holds some fascination for him. He receives few visitors at Gorki. His third secretary at Party headquarters, Kaganovitch, his fellow Georgian, Ordzhonikidze and Mikoyan are almost the only communists invited to this retreat.

He is now, since so much more depends on him, much more protected than he was. Fifteen agents of the G.P.U. guard the house. The road from Gorki to Moscow is constantly watched by police and detectives. Each morning punctually at nine o'clock he sets off in a glittering Rolls-Royce with two guards on the step and a police automobile following. He has a long working day and only gets back home late at night. And after supper he commonly goes on working. He does not play cards like most of the other leaders and also, unlike other comrades, takes little pleasure in sitting round a table drinking and gossiping.

In the winter he moves his family back to the Kremlin, to his rooms there. That is less comfortable, but perhaps more to his liking. He engages no cook. The meals are sent in on a tray from the Communal restaurant. It is true he dines more amply than the working man; he does not stint his stomach. He has his mince stewed in grape leaves, his *shashlik*, his cranberry crème, all washed down with abundant wine from his native Georgia. He is not a vodka drinker and does not care for beer. Red table-wine

such as one can get at any *dukhan* in the Caucasus,
is all he asks. He enjoys good health; his abdominal
trouble does not recur.

The dinner is served on nationalised plates, some
of them still bearing the initials of the Tsars. His
rooms are simply furnished; no armchairs, divans
or anything of the kind; white-curtained windows;
wooden chairs; no tablecloth; a portrait of Lenin.
He sits down to dinner in the afternoon and to
supper in the evening with his new young consort,
Nadia, and his children. There are seldom any
visitors at these meals. Stalin eats and drinks and
says little. He does not discuss politics with his wife
nor tell her the events of the day. When the meal is
over he moves back his chair, lights his pipe and
seems to fall into a reverie. No one knows whether
on these occasions he is thinking of affairs of State
or merely enjoying the warmth of his digestive
processes.

He sits brooding with the face of a sphinx. An involuntary admirer of Stalin describes it in this way:

"Calm and immobile sits Stalin, with the stone face
of a prehistoric dragon, in which alone the eyes are
living. His thoughts, wishes, plans crowd upon his
mind. . . . He knows all that is happening in the
spaces of immense Russia. But nothing agitates him.
He has no doubts."[1]

Other observers of the dictator are inclined to
sneer. According to them his mind is a blank. He
is an opportunist who only thinks when something
arises which calls for action on his part. According
to them he is as economical in mental effort as he is
in speech.

[1] S. Dmitrievsky.

But Stalin has great power of mental concentration. He went through a test of a kind once. It was before the revolution. The Tsar's police and military were tired of his constant escapes from banishment and decided to put him through a torture which few survive with sanity. He was made to run the gauntlet of the Salyansky regiment and each soldier beat him as he passed with the butt end of his rifle. Stalin concentrated his thoughts upon some aspect of Marxism, gritted his teeth and walked the whole alley of yelling and buffeting soldiers. The man who could do that has some almost Indian power of thought over body. So one need not assume that in his long silences over his pipe Stalin has not thought out the development of the revolution and the next steps in his career.

It is noticeable that he prizes and protects his privacy. In his home he is immune from unwanted visitors or telephone calls. It is more difficult to get to see him in his Kremlin retreat than it was to see Lenin. And he cannot be called up by troublesome citizens on the telephone. The important people of the regime have their own limited telephone exchange. Thus a call on one of the telephones in Stalin's apartments can only proceed from one of his associates. According to one of the secretaries, there is an apparatus which is only used for listening in to other members' conversation. He is watchful. The power which he has won it is his intention to keep. A telephone message from him to the G.P.U. disposes of the freedom, perhaps of the life, of any individual in all Russia. The Tsars were as absolute, but their power was not so great.

When Stalin gained the supreme control for

which he had worked certain more unsympathetic traits in his character manifested themselves. He became more reserved, more difficult of access, less social. He is friendly with only those who are useful to him. With others, if they pester him or make up to him, he is upon occasion very rude, letting loose foul language to which there is no reply. Yet this roughness is broken now and again by some ray of peasant heartiness. A comrade gets ill: he sends him a barrel of honey. "Hey, eat this and get well!" he writes.

While Stalin is not popular he is a hero to Red youth. The attitude toward him is compounded of admiration and dread. Everyone knows he is no charlatan, that he is politically uncorruptible, that he will not sell the revolution. And those who have to deal with him know that he is clever and capable. What holds many to him who might otherwise prove disloyal is the belief that if he falls everything goes with him. The rest make their speeches and carry out his instructions, but he is the Man of the Revolution. At a meeting, be it of the *Sovnarkom* or of Communist Youth, or of any other body, there is the characteristic Slavonic air of unreality and ineffectiveness until Stalin comes into the hall. When he makes his entry, even though he may not be going to utter a word, backs straighten, attentiveness concentrates; the audience is in the presence of the great leader, reality has entered.

When he speaks it is with a strong Georgian accent. His speeches are written and he stares at his manuscript while he reads. As an orator he would be ineffective but for the fascination of his personality and his sharp unexpected gestures. His speeches

are lengthy but not verbose. The wording is succinct
and direct. They make better reading than the
speeches of Lenin and Trotsky because they are
informed more by purpose than by theory. Yet
there is a curious disparity between his speeches
and his conversation, the one so discursive and
urbane, the other so sparse and rough.

He is not an emotional man like Roosevelt, nor
does he live on his nerves like Lloyd George or
MacDonald. He has nerves, he can get excited, but
he is always under control. His nerves are not
frayed by the difficulties of administration. He
leaves administration to his subordinates. He reserves
to himself direction, judgment and power itself. He
commonly makes subordinates responsible for the
advice they give him. "What do you think ought to
be done? Well, go and do it!" At times he breaks
through some wordy confusion of the underlings
with a plain command, as in the case when the
Labour Government of Great Britain was disposed
to grant a resumption of diplomatic relationship on
certain terms. Stalin had no doubt about that. If there
was a chance to re-establish the prestige of British
recognition, he knew of no objections in the matter of
promises or terms. He heard what the Foreign
Commissary and his colleagues had to say against it,
and just made one comment in his characteristic
brutal way, "Chepukha!" which is the Russian
equivalent of "Balderdash!"

Stalin's government became represented at St.
James's and in due course the pathetic, self-pitying
Trotsky, shivering in Constantinople, was refused
the right of asylum in Great Britain which he
claimed.

One weakness of the isolation of Stalin is that his executive does not always tell him the truth. He can be explosive upon the receipt of unpleasant news, and rather than risk his anger his agents deceive him sometimes. According to Bessedovsky that is especially true of his ambassadors and foreign ministers. Bessedovsky is the envoy to France who barricaded himself in his embassy and then went over to the other side. He may be prejudiced, but in his memoirs he seems to be a fair man. According to him he mortally annoyed Stalin by reporting a Communist demonstration in Paris in these terms: "On the 1st of August on the streets of Paris 2,000 workmen came out on parade accompanied by 20,000 police." On receipt of this message an agent of the G.P.U. was at once despatched to Paris to order Bessedovsky to return forthwith to Moscow for party trial. Be that as it may, Stalin seems generally to be well informed, judging from the statements in his speeches.

Isolation also brings with it the danger of assassination. There is always the temptation to kill a man who has gathered all power into his own hands. Great confusion would be caused in Russia if Stalin died prematurely. Such a will as his is rare and could not be replaced by mere administrative ability such as Molotof possesses. "If Stalin dies the system collapses" is a common saying.

He has attracted to himself much political hate. A man who has so cleverly disposed of his rivals cannot be safe from the motive of revenge. The chief precaution against that is the ceaseless vigilance of the G.P.U. and of Stalin himself. It is even dangerous to whisper against Stalin: the very walls have ears. The chief deterrent is the knowledge that an abortive plot on Stalin's life would be visited by a terrible vengeance. Stalin is not wantonly cruel, but he is not soft or sentimental, nor just nor legalistic. The telephone and the executioner form his measure of law.

CHAPTER XVI

THE Five Year Plan may easily stretch on to be a Ten Year Plan. The plan itself and not the time limit is important. "We are fifty or a hundred years behind the leading countries of the world" said Stalin. "We must cover that distance in ten years. Either that, or we shall be swept away."

That same Fifteenth Congress which excluded the whole Trotsky faction and prefaced Trotsky's banishment, promulgated and approved the Five Year Scheme which had been drawn up by the Gosplan in the early months of 1927. It was a plan to increase industrial production 78 per cent and agricultural production 30 per cent during the period 1928–1933. This ambitious calculation was based on the possibility of turning to account the enormous natural resources of Russia properly exploited by machinery and disciplined labour.

The agricultural output was to be achieved by the State farms and the collectives using the tractor and the harvester. The scheme for industry was of necessity more elaborate. Russia has for long been a great agricultural country. Before the war she was also a great producer of raw materials but she has never been industrialised like Britain or Germany. The Plan called for the rehabilitation of old factories and the building of new ones, the purchase on an enormous scale of new equipment abroad, day and night operation of the factories and the workshops, an eight hour working day with three shifts of workmen. Thousands of skilled foreigners were to be brought in to superintend the new works.

None of this could have fructified without the will of Stalin behind it. A new Peter the Great had arisen and again the Russian millions were going to be made to work. It is sometimes said rather foolishly that we need a Five Year Plan in England, but there is a great difference between industrial Russia and industrial England. At present no one can be forced to work and operate a scheme devised by politicians. The Russian leaders have no Trade Union rules to embarrass them, or if there are Trade Union rules they can be altered at will to suit the exigencies of the situation. Underfed, ill clothed, ill paid, the millions are driven to work. No union has power to prevent piece-work or competitive working. The foremen and the police deal rigorously with "ca-canny," which is apt to be labelled with the unpleasanter name of sabotage. Hundreds have been shot and thousands banished for attempting to make others go slowly.

The development is not only important to the Russian republic but to the whole Western world. Scoffed at in 1928 as a gigantic bluff, the Plan had made sufficient progress in 1930 for every capitalistic state to take cognizance of it. The question then posed in all seriousness was: "Can it succeed?" Still doubts were expressed, but speculation as to the result gave way to apprehension. For while Russia was building up phenomenally, the capitalistic system of the West seemed to be breaking down.

The first object of the Plan is to support and facilitate large scale agriculture, not only to employ machinery but to make it and thus be independent of import. The second object is to make Russia self-supporting in manufacture. The third is to improve the living conditions of the population as a whole, and the fourth is to prove by example and economic war that Capitalism is out of date and must be supplanted by the Russian system, call it Marxian if you will.

So they have the Selmashtroy works for turning out agricultural implements and machinery near Rostof; the Stalingrad tractor factory planned to turn out fifty thousand tractors a year; the Nizny Novgorod factory for motor trucks and cars. As constructional steel is necessary for the factories of an American type springing up all over the land they have started the immense steel works at Magneti-gorsk. As coal in ever-increasing quantities is required modern coal cutting machinery has been installed in the old mines and new fields have been opened up. Molotof, who in himself is the supreme executive of the Five Year Plan, declares that up to October, 1930, he had started 323 new factories.[1]

The cotton growing in Turkestan has been largely extended, and the Moscow factories re-equipped and new mills constructed. Working the mills to capacity, day and night, meant a tremendous requirement of raw cotton, something far in excess of what Turkestan could supply. Even large purchases of American bales have not kept the machines going all the time. The new asbestos spinning mills in the Urals are in this respect better circumstanced.

In the cotton spinning industry the war on the capitalist system seems to have taken precedence of the clothing of the ragged populations at home.

[1] V. M. Molotof: *The Success of the Five Year Plan.*

The export of manufactured cotton cannot be easily frustrated by an embargo or a hostile tariff. Its chief outlet is not Europe but Asia. At least half of the cotton manufactured is designed to be sold in China and the East. While the Indian boycott is one cause of Lancashire's inactivity the invasion of the rest of Asia by the Russian product is overlooked. Politically also, Moscow, in aiding and abetting Indian nationalism in which it does not necessarily believe, has done much to help the cotton boycott. And in fomenting disturbance in Eastern China, Moscow has successfully reserved the whole of the interior for her trade. In the case of cotton, Britain is in a state of economic war with Russia and being worsted in the fight.

In the matter of grain export, the war is upon the United States, Canada and certain small states of Central Europe such as Hungary. The defence of the Soviet regime in the case of cotton as in the case of grain, is that it sells in order to buy and import the machinery and equipment necessary for the realisation of the Plan.

The early stages of transition in this economic revolution in the life of Russia were marked by much unrest and rebelliousness. Even the politicians were disturbed by the hurly burly into which their destiny seemed to have been thrown. Some were in favour of slackening down and giving the Plan more time, but Stalin opposed compromise.

"Many are of opinion that our economic backwardness might be overcome at a quieter tempo," said he. "They do not like the mad pace at which we are going, the harnessing of all the resources of the country, the staking of everything on one

card. Sometimes it is asked, could we not slow
down somewhat? No, that is impossible, comrades.
It is impossible to reduce the tempo. On the contrary,
as occasion offers, we must increase it."

The reason which Stalin gives for the Five Year
Plan is that a psychological moment had arrived.
Either Russia must make herself completely independent in an economic sense or she must go under,
the proletarian revolution must fail. He quotes the
words of Lenin:—"We must either overtake the
capitalistic countries or perish."

"To reduce the tempo means to lag behind and
the laggards get killed," said Stalin. "But we do not
wish to be beaten. No, we do not wish it! The
history of Russia is an uninterrupted procession of
defeats due to backwardness. We were beaten by
the Mongol khans, by the Turkish beys, by the
feudal Swedes, by the Polish—by the Poles and
Lithuanians, by the Anglo-French capitalists, by
the Japanese barons. And all because of backwardness. Because of backwardness and out of date
methods of agriculture. . . . The law of capitalism
is the wolf's law. You lag behind, you are weak,
that must mean you are in the wrong and can be
devoured. But if you are powerful that means you
are in the right and others must be on their guard.
For that reason it is impossible for us to remain
backward any more."

The realisation of the Plan has therefore gone on
at the first hot pace, if anything a little accelerated.
A feature of further development and progress is
the educational advance, the establishment of many
schools and polytechnics for training skilled artisans
and engineers in the hope of replacing the immense

foreign service by skilled Russians. That however is a far view and does not relate to the immediate exigencies of the situation.

The most successful of all undertakings has proved to be that of the Soviet farms, which have done much better than the collectives. Their grain production has exceeded the estimate by 100 per cent. One of these "Gigant" which covers an area of 500,000 acres is one of the wonders of the agricultural world and has been visited by over 50,000 people who came to observe or gaze. Most of these farms are of enormous extent; many of them are on virgin soil. When all those planned have been organised it is calculated that their gross area will exceed that of the grain producing land of Canada by one million hectares.

These State farms are run of economic lines, being unhampered by an enormous mass of supernumerary peasant hands which the collectives have not yet been able to dispose of. If the grain production of the collective exceeds that of the State farms it must be remembered that on the latter more people have to be fed.

Molotof gives remarkable figures of the absorption of individual farms by the collectives:

Date	Number of individual farms absorbed by the collectives	Percentage of all farms.
1st October, 1927	286,000	1.1
,, 1928	595,000	2.3
,, 1929	2,131,000	8.1
,, 1930	5,565,000	22.2
1st March, 1931	8,830,000	35.3

Already the collective farms of Russia have as large an area sown as that of France and Italy put together. According to Stalin the gross output of grain by the collective farms was multiplied fifty-fold during the first three years of the Plan. The area sown now more than doubles the area envisaged by the Plan. If the success is maintained Russia must very shortly dominate the grain market of the world.

Industrialisation, to some extent attendant upon agriculture, has also made giant strides which are the more remarkable in view of Russia's great backwardness and tempermental incapacity for industry. To some extent the foreign contractors, engineers and foremen are responsible for this success. We must add the unique manœuvre of employing what are known as "shock brigades" of workers to go and speed matters up whenever a factory showed signs of lagging behind the set programme. Some hundreds of these brigades have been enrolled. The members are mostly ardent young Communists, their activity may be regarded as the antithesis of the Trade Union spirit. They break up the principle of "ca-canny" where they find it in practice. They denounce the inefficient and the recalcitrant. They start competitions as to which gang of workmen will do the most work in an hour or a day. They are responsible for the black lists and red lists appearing in the newspapers. Those who are not "doing their bit" find their names pilloried in the Press, which is neither pleasant nor safe. On the other hand the heroes of the workshop are enrolled in the red lists with stars for commendation. In this way an enthusiasm for the realisation of the Five Year Plan in industry has been enkindled and made nation-wide.

Stalin gives the following remarkable figures of the growth of industry:

In 1926–7, we had in the whole of industry, both large and small scale, reckoning also flour milling, a gross output of 8,641 million pre-war roubles, *i.e.* 102.5 per cent of the pre-war level. The following year we had 122 per cent. In 1928–9 we had 142.5 per cent and in the current year (estimated) not less than 180 per cent of the pre-war level.[1]

During the same period the freight carried on the railroads increased by 66 per cent. Railway construction increased considerably, likewise bridge construction. The whole commercial turnover doubled. Foreign trade, exports and imports, which in 1927–8 was only 47.9 per cent of the pre-war total, increased to about 80 per cent. The average yearly increase in the national income during the first three years of the Five Year Plan amounted to 15 per cent.

These are all figures quoted by Stalin himself and there is no reason to think them materially inaccurate. Foreign observers of the immense activity might have been tempted to estimate the actual success in more rosy terms. Stalin is a stickler for facts, and window-dressing is not a feature of his political life.

The triumph of Stalin in the Five Year Plan lies in the fact that the Bolsheviks are taking over the whole of Russia economically as they had taken her over politically. Before the Plan there existed the anomaly of a great deal of private ownership and some capitalistic enterprise existing side by side with

[1] J. Stalin: *Political Report to the XVIth Party Congress.*

proletarian socialism. The Five Year Plan was almost worth inaugurating for the victory over the peasant alone. But also in the industrial field it has made its conquests. Petty private trading has been engulfed by the State undertakings and the concessions held by foreign financial groups and companies have languished in these years. According to Stalin, capital investment in private property declined nearly 20 per cent in the first three years of the Plan. The socialistic, large scale State undertakings in industry amounted in 1930 to 99 per cent of the whole.

In March, 1931, at the ten year anniversary of the introduction of the N.E.P. Molotof reviewed the Five Year Plan at the sixth Congress of the *Sovnarkom* in the Grand Opera House in Moscow. There he laid some stress upon this political victory. There had been two lines of thought regarding the development of the New Economic Policy. Stalin holds that Lenin never intended the N.E.P. to be extended along capitalist lines. "The N.E.P. was so designed that in the course of an initial retreat, we may regroup our forces and then resume the offensive."[1]

But Trotsky, and, at times, Kamenef and Zinovief and the Menshevik faction were for the extension of the N.E.P. by the parcelling out of the resources of Russia to foreign groups, consortiums of Russian and foreign capital such as that formed to operate the Lena Goldfields. Despite the prominence of Stalin all the while since Lenin's death the programme of seeking the co-operation of international capital in Russia became sufficiently advanced for foreign observers to surmise that the revolution would go capitalist after all. The proletarian dictatorship would

[1] J. Stalin: *Leninism.*

be rotted from within. But Stalin was in reality opposed to the N.E.P. from the start, and during all the years of the struggle with Trotsky and the Right and Left wing factions in the Party sought the power to return to the militant communism of the first years of the revolution.

Molotof stated the new situation in clear terms, addressing the *Sovnarkom*:

It has been our task to carry out the policy of the N.E.P. on Bolshevik lines. Our foes calculated on the carrying out of the N.E.P. on Menshevik, that is capitalist lines. An irreconcilable struggle has been carried on all over the world between these two political lines. This has not ceased to-day. The essence of the struggle is as follows: Our party has staked, and continues to stake all on the victory of Socialism and on the annihilation of the remnants of capitalism. Our enemies have staked on the bourgeois degeneration of the Soviet Union and on the destruction of the Socialist elements. . . . The victory has gone to the Leninist policy, the policy of irreconcilable struggle against Trotskyism and the Right tendency, which expressed the bourgeois influence on some small strata of the vanguard of the proletariat.[1]

Some of the proletarian comrades asked for the final abolition of the N.E.P. but Stalin called that stupidity. "The N.E.P. was introduced to bring about the victory of Socialism over the capitalist elements. In passing to the offensive of Socialism along the whole front, we are still not abolishing the N.E.P., for private trade and capitalist elements still remain, commodity circulation and money economy still remain: but we are certainly abolishing the initial stage of the N.E.P., developing its further stage, the present stage of the N.E.P., which is its final stage."

[1] V. M. Molotof: *The Success of the Five Year Plan.*

CHAPTER XVII

THERE are no rich: only the State gets rich. On the other hand there are innumerable poor and the betterment of their conditions is a promise, not a realisation. Culture is almost dead. The most is made of the Moscow theatres but there were always interesting theatres in Moscow. The religious side of the Russian nature has almost been eclipsed. Visitors say there are just as many people in the churches as ever, but they have little means of judging. The removal of the Iverska shrine, the destruction of the beautiful cathedral of St. Saviour, the largest in Moscow, are signs of the times. It is absurd to call Communism a religion; no religion can be based on materialism. For religion in itself means a disbelief in the validity of materialism.

Nevertheless we have the agreeable spectacle of a whole nation at work. Russia at the bidding of a great materialist has risen out of the sloth of the ages. It used to be a saying before the revolution: "Russia's day is coming, not to-morrow, but the day after to-morrow". The day after to-morrow seems to be arriving ahead of time. It was also said: " The hegemony of the races will pass from the Anglo-Saxon to the Russian." Throughout the stormy years of the revolution, it has not looked like it until now. At the same time it may be observed that Russia's day was always thought to be one in which Science, Art and Letters would shine and the leadership would not be merely one of production, trade and politics. Religion and idealism entered very considerably into the vision.

But Russia is rising, not in friendly rivalry but in stark opposition. Her success is viewed not with admiration but with apprehension, as if another Attila were threatening the civilisation of the West. Almost the only vital questions which are pressed are: "Does it mean war? Does it mean universal revolution?"

It is not outside the bounds of possibility that Stalin may become the Dictator of Europe or that the elastic U.S.S.R. may be very considerably extended.

"The tide has turned," said Stalin addressing the Party. "The tide has turned not only for us but also for the capitalist countries of the whole world. While for us the turn has meant a new and more important economic *advance*, for the capitalist countries it has meant a turn towards economic *decline*. We in the U.S.S.R. have a *growing advance* in socialist construction, both in industry and in agriculture. They, the capitalists, have a *growing crisis* in their economic life, both in industry and in agriculture."

While the West suffers from over-production and is being forced to destroy its surpluses in order to keep up prices, Russia is aggravating the situation by intensifying production. The unemployed of the Western nations have ceased to be a labour reserve and have become a standing army. A world revolutionary element has come into being through the existence of many millions of poverty-stricken toilers. The advice given to the Farm Board in America to burn the 275 millions of bushels of unsaleable wheat it has on its hand and the advice given to the cotton planters to plough in a considerable fraction of their cotton shows the inability of Western economists to grapple with a problem which is ultimately not one of prices but of politics.

Stalin says: "A system of economy does not know what to do with its surplus output and can only burn it, at a time when the masses are in the grip of want and unemployment, hunger and misery—such a system of economy passes the death sentence on itself."

The social services which do much to render the condition of the poor more tolerable depend on taxation and must naturally fall into decay when taxation fails to produce the amount necessary to support them.

The Red leaders view the situation from their vantage ground of the Kremlin with considerable complacency. Capitalism seems of itself to be falling to the ground as Marx said it would. But their enterprise, Russian revolutionary socialism, is in full swing, and helping to bring about the Western débâcle. "History must be given a shove" and they are shoving.

Stalin, however, sees war first before revolution, not war between the U.S.S.R. and any other country but internecine war among the capitalist nations. "The bourgeois States are furiously arming. What for? Of course, not for a friendly talk, but for war. The imperialists need war because it is the only means of dividing up the world afresh, dividing up anew the markets, sources of raw material and spheres for capital investment. In such conditions so-called Pacifism is living out its last days, the League of Nations is rotting even before burial, 'disarmament schemes' are falling into oblivion, while conferences for reducing naval armaments become conferences for re-equipping and extending navies. This means that the war danger will grow at an increasingly rapid rate."

But the international policy of the U.S.S.R. remains pacific, not pacific as regards economics and politics but pacific as regards military invasion of other lands. As Stalin says with some pride: "We have our own technique."

Nevertheless, we cannot but surmise, that in the event of a European war, Russia would not escape being embroiled. If, as is not unlikely, Germany will make a bid to recover her lost territory, will Russia not be allured by the pleasant prospect of trouncing the Poles or of re-annexing their lost but much regretted Bessarabia? Or if such a war should develop, according to plan, into a revolutionary civil war, should we not find Red Russia lending a bayonet? There is no Pacifism in the U.S.S.R. It is founded upon war; it preaches war all the time, class-war. And Stalin's Russia would not be found in a state of unpreparedness. The new industrialism provides great scope for the mass manufacture of munitions and engines of war.

The dictator is, however, a cool and crafty politician. He has a genius for doing the right thing at the right time. He is no hot-head. He does not crave glory. If the West will destroy itself he will let the West do the work for the Party. He will do his utmost to keep the country out of a destructive war, especially in these years of growth and reorganisation. But he is not working for Russia alone, or even merely for himself. He does envisage world revolution and keeps the forces at his command headed for it all the while.

One Russian writer goes further than I do in his description of Russia under the Five Year Plan. Perhaps he goes too far, but the picture is striking and gives one pause:

"The hammer blows are falling. Human arms are harnessed. The machines revolve. . . . New houses are springing up, whole new cities. The earth is broken and gives new streams of naphtha, metals, coal. The sirens are howling from one new State farm after another. Machines give birth to machines. The factory gates open and there crawl out and range themselves in threatening ranks armoured cars, tanks, guns, aeroplanes. They bear out stacks of as yet silent rifles, millions of cold bayonets. Millions of shells. Melancholy rows of cylinders of poison gases. How much strength, how much precious metal, how many million pounds of bread, how much thought and human muscle went to the creation of all that? And all of that is little! Machines beget machines, and chiefly machines for the destruction of other people. Every blow of a hammer, every revolution of a wheel seems to say:—'Give us Europe!'

"At times instead of tanks, it is tractors and ploughs. They break through the black earth, they raise the as yet unploughed steppe. They raise grain which will again be converted into machines, guns, gas. The Volkhof station works smoothly. The dams of Dneiprshtroy are being built. The Svirshtroy is rising. An arc lamp blazes where but yesterday it was the moon. A new system of irrigation is watering the deserts of Central Asia. New mountains of raw cotton hurtle toward the greedy jaws of the mills. Thence roll out long kilometres of manufactured cotton. It is packed and sent abroad to be sold in exchange for machines for making machines, and for inventions affording a better means of killing other people. . . . Magnetoshtroy is growing. The coal fields of the Kuznetsk basin are being extended. Soon

Siberian coal and Ural ore will unite, for the making of new machines and engines of war. . . . The Turksib is developing. A canal to join the Volga and the Don is planned. Thousands of new things are being planned. The combination of these things must raise Russia to a height as yet unknown, and throw down the West into the mud."[1]

Doubtless that is much too much to say. Yet no one knows the mind of Stalin. His speeches, one of which often makes a fair-sized book, are largely prepared by his secretaries. They review a situation which is already known and do not speculate as to a situation which may arise. He is an opportunist. He has always watched tendency and followed it. He has converted Russia into one great powerful self-increasing mechanism. In that respect the economy of the new Russia has something in common with the Capitalist system at which he jeers. Capitalism is also mechanical and either ceaselessly expands or collapses. The Marxian formula that Capitalism bears in itself the germ of its own destruction is perhaps true of the system inaugurated in Russia. It must go on. "Either we go on or we shall fall to ruin," Stalin himself confesses. How like Capitalism! The new mechanism of the Five Year Plan goes on and when it tops a hill Stalin will be there to describe the new landscape to the Party. Then it will devour that landscape, Stalin following. And rising to another crest, Stalin will be there to describe another vista to the Party. But into what new land is this mechanism leading them . . . not into Europe?

The outstanding talent of Stalin is his ability to tell the executive, the experts, the groups what is

[1] S. Dmitrievsky; *Stalin.*

next to be done and how to set about it. He has
been stronger than Lenin but he has added nothing
to Leninism except tactics; add of course will, vigilance and judgment of character. He is a general
of the economic and political revolution. Without
him the machine would go on, but the Five Year
Plan would probably end in a fiasco. Stalin enjoys
a dangerous isolation in leadership. He has harnessed
the young, the eager, the ardent and has displaced
the older and more experienced men. Molotof,
his second in command, is likely to inherit his power,
And Molotof is reputed to be hard and to have a
strong will, but he lacks the sagacity of Stalin.
Even with Stalin in control, the way forward for
Russia is beset with difficulties.

It is true that the crisis in the capitalist regime
of the nations of the West cheers the counsels of
Communism. But the balance between the destinies
of Capitalism and Communism is fine. It would
have been easier for Russia if the depression had
been deferred for two or three years. In the Five
Year Plan Communism has profited largely by the
markets of the capitalistic West. But these markets
are failing prematurely through over-production.
The Farm Board of America with its 275,000 bushels
of surplus wheat may knock the bottom out of the
grain market just when Russia is preparing to do
so with her own surplus. If Russia begins to fail
to get a good price for her surpluses of food and
raw materials she will be hampered in her purchases
of machinery.

The Five Year Plan has been greatly extended
since its conception. It now envisages a stupendous
expansion. Much depends on the punctual fulfil-

ment of each item on the schedule. If one section gets behind it puts the whole out of gear. But punctuality does not entirely depend on the enthusiasm of the workers and the will of Stalin. The stability of foreign markets is an important element of success. The Plan contains a cash nexus with the West. An increasing amount of money must be raised each year by selling produce to the West. If that is not realised the buying programme has to be curtailed. Equipment, due to arrive on a specified date at the vast shells of new factories built on American lines, is not there on time and the whole work is held up. There is still a risk that the economic crash in the West may ruin the Five Year Plan, and that the Russia of a few years' time may be a land of strange, derelict factories, and that the expansion may prove to have been one of the greatest commercial and financial bubbles in history.

The least likely thing to fail is the new mechanised farming for which Russia is so admirably suited. That, even if curtailed somewhat in extent, is likely to survive any crash. Despite the prognostications of pessimistic economists, a pleasant dénouement is not improbable. Russia will at last be unable to sell abroad her vast surpluses of wheat and they will roll back on the stinted populations bringing prosperity and comfort. Stalin would then fall but that would not matter much. He would have had his day.

BIBLIOGRAPHY

Contemporaries, by M. A. Aldanof. (Contains a good essay on Stalin, but has not as yet been translated into English.)

Remarks of a Previous Assistant of Stalin, by Boris Bazhanof.

Avec Staline dans le Kremlin.

Stalin, by Bessedovsky and Laporte. (In preparation.)

Stalin, S. Dmitrievsky.

Lenin, by D. S. Mirsky.

The Five Year Plan, by V. M. Molotof.

The New Phase in the Soviet Union, by V. M. Molotof.

Leninism, by J. Stalin.

Political Report to the XVIth Party Congress, by J. Stalin.

Marxism and the National Question, by J. Stalin.

My Life, by Leon Trotsky.

Stalin and the Red Army, by K. Voroshilof. (Included in a symposium on Stalin, edited by Naganovitch.)

INDEX